Anatol Lieven and John Hulsman

ETHICAL REALISM

Anatol Lieven is chair of international relations and terrorism studies in the War Studies Department of King's
College London and a senior fellow of the New America
Foundation. He is the author of *America Right or Wrong:
An Anatomy of American Nationalism* (2004), and is a
regular contributor to the *Financial Times* and the *International Herald Tribune*, among other publications.

John Hulsman is a former senior research fellow at The
Heritage Foundation. A member of the Council on Foreign Relations, he is also contributing editor to *The
National Interest*. He advises congressional leaders from
both parties on foreign policy issues and makes regular
appearances on ABC, CBS, Fox News, CNN, MSNBC,
PBS, and the BBC. He lives in Culpeper, Virginia.

ETHICAL REALISM

A VISION FOR AMERICA'S ROLE
IN THE WORLD

Anatol Lieven and John Hulsman

VINTAGE BOOKS
A Division of Random House, Inc.
New York

FIRST VINTAGE BOOKS EDITION, NOVEMBER 2007

The Library of Congress has cataloged the Pantheon edition as follows:
Lieven, Anatol.
Ethical realism : a vision for America's role in the world /
by Anatol Lieven and John Hulsman.
p.   cm.
Includes bibliographical references.
1. United States—Foreign relations—2001– 2. Moral realism.
I. Hulsman, John. II. Title.
JZ1480.L56 2006   172'.40973—dc22   2006043673

VINTAGE ISBN: 978-0-307-27738-1

Author photograph © Claudio Vazquez
Book design by M. Kristen Bearse

www.vintagebooks.com

Printed in the United States of America
10 9 8 7 6 5 4 3 2 1

For Sasha, Misha, Heather, and Benjamin,
with our love

God of our fathers, known of old—
    Lord of our far-flung battle line
Beneath whose awful hand we hold
    Dominion over palm and pine—
Lord God of Hosts, be with us yet,
Lest we forget—lest we forget!

The tumult and the shouting dies;
    The captains and the kings depart:
Still stands Thine ancient sacrifice,
    An humble and a contrite heart.
Lord God of Hosts, be with us yet,
Lest we forget—lest we forget!

Far-called, our navies melt away;
    On dune and headland sinks the fire:
Lo, all our pomp of yesterday
    Is one with Nineveh and Tyre!
Judge of the Nations, spare us yet,
Lest we forget—lest we forget!

If, drunk with sight of power, we loose
    Wild tongues that have not Thee in awe—
Such boasting as the Gentiles use
    Or lesser breeds without the law—
Lord God of Hosts, be with us yet,
Lest we forget—lest we forget!

For heathen heart that puts her trust
    In reeking tube and iron shard—
All valiant dust that builds on dust,
    And guarding, calls not Thee to guard—
For frantic boast and foolish word,
Thy mercy on Thy people, Lord!

—RUDYARD KIPLING,
"Recessional," 1897

Contents

Introduction

The price of greatness is responsibility.
—WINSTON CHURCHILL

What has failed in Iraq has been not just the strategy of the administration of George W. Bush, but a whole way of looking at the world. This consists of the beliefs that America is both so powerful and so obviously good that it has the ability to spread democracy throughout the world; that if necessary, this can be achieved through war; that this mission can also be made to advance particular U.S. national interests; and that this combination will naturally be supported by good people all over the world, irrespective of their own political traditions, national allegiances, and national interests.

These beliefs are very widely and instinctively shared throughout the U.S. establishment and both political parties. As a result, their failure in Iraq has so far led not to a new approach to international relations, but to a period of intellectual and political bewilderment. This is now being succeeded by worrying indications of an emerging new bipartisan consensus, based essentially on the previous assumptions and myths.

Even after the debacle of Iraq, there is therefore at present no real opposition in America when it comes to foreign and security policy. The Democrats are bitterly, and rightly, critical of the monstrous incompetence displayed by the Bush administration. But they do not themselves have an alternative strategy or philosophy to offer, and too often content themselves with offering similar

messianic platitudes about American greatness and the transfor-
mative power of democracy.

Thus Senator Hillary Rodham Clinton of New York, in a speech
at Princeton in January 2006, essentially took the same line as
the Bush administration's National Security Strategy—NSS—two
months later. She called for a tough line on Iraq, declared that
democracy—and not new diplomacy—is the solution to the Middle
East's conflicts, and used the same naive and utopian language as
the administration:

> History can be like a yoke around a people's neck. History can blind
> you to the possibilities that lie ahead if you're just able to break free
> and take that step. . . . It can get better, just get over it. Make a deci-
> sion for hope, make a decision for peace. Create a new reality.[1]

The message from too many Democrats and Republicans alike
remains that we should not let facts get in the way of our day-
dreams. It's so much easier to fantasize about an alternative and
ideal world, rather than making the hard and unpopular decisions
that are necessary to deal with the complicated and frustrating one
in which we live. It is so much easier to imagine that world as a
blank slate on which America can draw as it wishes, rather than to
recognize the limits on American power, and recalibrate strategy
accordingly. If Americans fail to reexamine their fundamental attitudes toward that world, then the risk for the future is that failure
in Iraq will make the United States more cautious, but not wiser.

We have been through this cycle before.

Vietnam taught us once that the United States is not invincible.
All America's technological superiority, and all the courage and
skill of its soldiers, may be useless against certain kinds of enemies
using certain kinds of strategy. After all, military power is not
something you hang on a wall for visitors to admire; real military
power is power that can be used. America's famous twelve aircraft
carrier battle groups are not much use on the streets of Fallujah.
Vietnam also should have taught us that American preaching of

democracy—even with the best of intentions—will not be accepted by other peoples if it is accompanied by strategies that they see as opposed to their national pride and national aspirations. Yet, a generation later, these lessons seem to have been forgotten.

The stakes today are much higher than they were in Vietnam. Despite the illusions of that time, Indochina was never really very important to the United States, to its leadership in the world, or to the world economy. Nobody could say that of the Middle East today. Nor was there ever a chance of the Vietnamese Communists (or Saddam Hussein for that matter) attacking Americans at home. Americans, the British, and the Spanish all have bitter reason to know that this is not true of Al Qaeda and its allies.

The threat from Islamist terrorism has to be taken very seriously indeed—more seriously than any other security issue now facing the United States. Unfortunately, the left, believing the terrorist threat has been exaggerated, directs more of its attention and criticism at America's own government than at the nation's mortal enemies. Meanwhile, the Bush administration's war in Iraq has squandered time and energy, increased Muslim hatred of the United States, and created a breeding ground for terrorists. A war with Iran would repeat this dreadful mistake on an even larger scale.

Shunning these distractions, we need to focus on Al Qaeda and their allies in the world of Sunni Islamist extremism. These are the people who actually carried out 9/11 and killed thousands of Americans. They are seeking weapons of mass destruction, and if they gain them and can deploy them, they will carry out atrocities far worse than 9/11—and not just against us, but against all their enemies. Russians, Shia Muslims in Iraq and Pakistan, and victims of the Taliban in Afghanistan all have good reason to know this. The Islamist terrorists are also our most dangerous enemies because they can persuade us to destroy ourselves. We have already seen in the years after 9/11 how that terrorist attack has led our administration and military into actions and arguments that previous generations of Americans would have found inconceivable.

These actions have tarnished the image of American democracy in the world, and one shudders to think of the consequences for U.S. democracy of another truly massive terrorist attack.

A real threat demands a realistic response. Any approach to foreign policy that hopes to create an intellectual consensus in the United States must embrace certain elements of both realism and morality. For on the one hand, a majority of Americans have demonstrated repeatedly throughout modern history their aversion to strategies based purely on criteria of international morality or humanitarianism, in their insistence that foreign policy serve the interests and above all the safety of the United States. This insistence has gained still greater force after 9/11. Equally dominant strains in the American tradition have repeatedly shown a deep aversion to strategies based on a "classical" realism free of all moral constraints and aims. For many Americans, central to these moral aims is a desire to spread freedom and democracy in the world.

Neoconservatives and liberal hawks do try to balance realism and morality. They were among the first to recognize a crucial fact about the terrorist threat: The internal nature of foreign countries matters as never before to American security—because Islamist revolution and extremism flourish in failed states and collapsed societies. They are correct that a classically realist approach isn't sufficient to deal with this situation.

Their answers, however, go much too far in the contradictory directions of both hard-line realism and utopian morality—or rather, as we shall argue, pseudo-realism and pseudo-morality. In the years since 9/11, both neoconservatives and liberal hawks have sought to make democracy the central element in American strategy in the Muslim world. At the level of public discourse they have achieved tremendous success. But they haven't achieved success where it really matters, on the streets of Iraq and in the politics of the Middle East in general. Iraq is a shambles that has gravely weakened the United States. And across the Middle East, wherever and whenever Muslims have been allowed to vote, they have voted for Islamist parties with programs that are bitterly hostile to American interests. Meanwhile, by pursuing the old-fashioned siren song of rolling back Russia, containing China, threatening Iran, and maintaining American and Israeli hegemony over the Middle East, these neoconservatives and liberal hawks have added a range of states to the list of America's problems.

Instead of this unsuccessful approach we propose two linked alternatives: the philosophy of ethical realism, and the concept of the Great Capitalist Peace. Ethical realism was propounded in the past by some of the great figures of the American intellectual tradition, including Reinhold Niebuhr, Hans Morgenthau, and George Kennan, and draws on a tradition stretching back through Edmund Burke to St. Augustine.

Reinhold Niebuhr (1892–1971), whom Kennan called "the father of us all," was a Protestant minister and theologian committed to social and economic progress. The threat to Western democracy first from Nazi Germany, then from Joseph Stalin's Soviet Union, led him also to place anti-totalitarianism at the center of his thought. The combination of his religious, social, and foreign policy imperatives led to the philosophy of ethical realism.

In a different but related form, this philosophy was also espoused by Hans Morgenthau (1904–1980), the father of modern realist thought in the United States. Morgenthau's classic work, *Politics Among Nations* (1948), altered the way international relations was taught in the United States, as it put the pursuit of specific American national interests at the center of foreign policy analysis, while qualifying this by a strong commitment to ethical imperatives and restraints. A Jewish refugee from Nazi Germany, Morgenthau never tired of reminding his beloved adopted country of the dangers of nationalist messianism, a deeply evil variant of which he had witnessed himself.

George Kennan (1904–2005), for his part, was not only a profound thinker in his own right but also a famous U.S. diplomat, whose "Long Telegram" of 1946 set out the strategy of "containment" of the Soviet Union that would be followed in different forms by every administration until the end of the Cold War. Like his fellow ethical realists Niebuhr and Morgenthau, Kennan also became deeply disillusioned with much of later U.S. strategy, and in particular with its mixture of militarization and messianic belief in American superiority. Niebuhr, Morgenthau, and Kennan were all supporters of resisting Communist aggression in Korea, but all joined in strong opposition to the Vietnam War. Their voices have been largely, and hauntingly, absent from the present foreign policy debate.

The concept of the Great Capitalist Peace is based on ethical realist thought and directly echoes Kennan's and Morgenthau's concepts of international order and the moral purposes of diplomacy, especially U.S. diplomacy. It denotes a global order tacitly agreed to by all the major states of the world, an order that guarantees their truly vital interests. In the short to medium term, we believe that this is essential if these states are to succeed in containing the terrorism that threatens them all. The Great Capitalist Peace depends in part on American power, and on the ability of that power to guarantee peace and order in certain parts of the world. In general, however, both the real limits on American power and the need to accommodate the legitimate interests and ambitions of other states mean that in most areas the use of American power needs to be deliberately restrained. Instead of exercising this power in an unrestrained way, the United States should whenever possible work through regional concerts linking the most important states of a region.

As its name suggests, the idea of the Great Capitalist Peace is founded on the fact that at the start of the twenty-first century all the major states of the world are committed to some version of capitalist economics and an orderly world market. The elites of these states draw tremendous personal benefits from this global capitalist system, and should naturally be opposed to allowing rivalry among themselves to destroy that market. They also have a strong common interest in resisting threats to the present world system from terrorists, extremists, and revolutionaries. By accommodating other great powers when possible, the Great Capitalist Peace makes stakeholders of much of the world, thereby perpetuating a stable, and reasonably just, global order.

The Great Capitalist Peace strategy flows directly from the ethical realist philosophy. Ethical realism points toward an international strategy based on prudence; a concentration on possible results rather than good intentions; a close study of the nature, views, and interests of other states, and a willingness to accommodate them when possible; and a mixture of profound American patriotism with an equally profound awareness of the limits both on American power and on American goodness.

In ethical realism, a sense of national modesty and limits is linked to a capacity to see ourselves as a nation as others see us—a capacity that in everyday human morality and interaction is generally seen as positive and attractive, while its opposite is seen as not merely unattractive but also somewhat ridiculous. As Niebuhr put it, "Nations, as individuals, who are completely innocent in their self-esteem, are insufferable in their human contacts."[2] In international affairs, it is essential that we try to see ourselves as others do. We cannot demand that the rest of the world simply trust in our benevolence and intelligence. We cannot expect other nations to believe it is in their best interest to allow us to exercise unconstrained power. As Francis Fukuyama has pointed out, this is a trust that Americans would never for a second place in any other country—and rightly so.[3] Or as Edmund Burke warned more than two centuries ago, "Nothing is so fatal to a nation as an extreme of self-partiality, and the total want of consideration of what others will naturally hope or fear."[4]

Moreover, ethical realism demolishes the shabby argument now being put forth by former hard-line supporters of the Iraq War that we should excuse their responsibility for this disaster because their intentions were good. Neither in statecraft nor in common sense can good intentions be a valid excuse if accompanied by gross recklessness, carelessness, and indifference to the range of possible consequences. Such actions fail the test not only of general ethics, but also of the sworn moral commitment of state servants and elected officials to defend the interests of their peoples, and not simply to pursue at all costs their own ideas of morality—another central point in realist ethics.

Niebuhr wrote that the modern West thinks it "has an easy solution for the problems of anarchy and chaos on both the international and national levels of community, because of its fatuous and superficial view of man. It does not know that the same man who is ostensibly devoted to the 'common good' may have desires and ambitions, hopes and fears, which set him at variance with his neighbors."[5] Today, the "easy solution" being promoted by the Bush administration and the Democratic leadership is the idea that the spread of democracy will inevitably lead to international peace, economic development, and the acceptance of American hegemony.

Coming from old Anglo-American Christian and skeptical traditions, the Founders of the republic recognized that it is deeply unwise to place unlimited powers in any hands and expect innate human goodness to guarantee that they will not be abused. This prudent recognition is responsible for the checks and balances on power that are integral to the Constitution, and therefore to American democratic civilization and its shining example to the world.

When it comes to the unconstrained use of power in the world, most ordinary citizens are wiser than their national leaders. By early 2006, numerous opinion surveys were showing that large majorities of Americans are deeply concerned not only with the war in Iraq but with the entire strategy being followed by the Bush administration. Their elected representatives, and their political system, however, have so far failed to present a coherent and effective alternative to that strategy. We offer this book as our contribution to the creation of such an alternative.

A note about ourselves: We are two foreign policy thinkers from what are usually taken to be opposite camps who have come together in frustration at the current stasis in the American foreign policy debate, and the very dangerous courses being pursued by the Bush administration and supported by leading Democrats. Our cooperation is one sign of the bankruptcy of the traditional party divisions as a way of understanding the real policy differences and alternatives facing America today. We hope that it will encourage others to break out of their tribal straitjackets and to draw up radically new approaches that will challenge both party establishments and serve the vital interests of Americans and their allies.

The Washington foreign policy community has become a series of cottage industries, speaking only to those who are part of our immediate circle, becoming adept at magnifying small and unimportant differences between our tribes, and incapable of seeking either truly new policies or a desperately needed new national consensus. In this environment, one of the greatest absences is a perception that party differences no longer mean much when it comes to actual policies. Despite all the name-calling, both party leaderships share essentially the same bankrupt and dangerous philosophy, while radical and valuable alternatives to this philosophy are being put forward by dissidents in both party camps.

Perhaps the mixture of superficial squabbling and underlying conformism in the party establishments would be marginally acceptable if the past years had ushered in a golden age of policy analysis. But in the ten years before 9/11, while we told ourselves fairy stories about the end of history, about the inevitable triumph of liberal capitalism and democracy, Al Qaeda grew stronger, flying mostly below the radar. And if the dreadful lessons of both 9/11 and the Iraq War were not enough, in 2006 we once again see attention and resources being diverted away from the terrorist threat toward rivalry with Russia and China and possible war with Iran.

Our sense of the unbearable nature of the present situation has led us to formulate a common approach, though we come to it from different backgrounds. Anatol Lieven, currently a senior research fellow at the "radical centrist" New America Foundation in Washington, D.C., is a former British journalist stationed in the Muslim world and the former Soviet Union. He experienced both the "liberation" struggle waged by U.S.-backed Islamist mujahideen in Afghanistan in the 1980s, and the disastrous consequences of radical economic and political "reform" in Russia in the 1990s. Lieven became involved in the wider U.S. debate as a result of his intense opposition to the Bush administration's launch of the Iraq War, and its failure to seek Muslim allies in the war on terror. In part, this was due to fear as to the consequences of these disastrous policies not only for the United States, but also for his own country, Britain, whose fate has become entangled with that of America.

The two chief influences on his thought are the realist tradition in international affairs, and the socially and economically progressive (or "solidarist") Catholic culture in which he was raised. These traditions led him to a combination of a commitment to the improvement of the human condition with deep skepticism about its perfectibility; to a conviction of the necessity of international peace and order for human progress; and to a profound belief in the duty of the present generation to act as stewards for their descendants. This in turn naturally led him to concern about climate change, and to anger at the selfishness and moral frivolity in this regard of too many contemporary leaders and groups.

This mixture also brought him naturally to ethical realism, since this philosophy was largely formulated by a great (Protestant) theologian, Reinhold Niebuhr, and draws on a Christian intellectual tradition stretching back to Thomas Aquinas and Augustine. His attitudes were also deeply shaped by family experience of the great European catastrophes of the twentieth century, and by personal experience—while serving as a journalist—of disastrous upheavals and conflicts in various parts of the world.

John Hulsman was until recently senior research fellow for European affairs at one of the largest think tanks in the world, the

Heritage Foundation. A member of the Council on Foreign Relations, Hulsman is a contributing editor at *The National Interest* and is a leading voice of a new generation of post–Cold War foreign policy thinkers/practitioners currently coming into their own following the Iraq crisis.

In his position as senior fellow (he was with the Heritage Foundation from 1999 to 2006), Hulsman was called on to construct and communicate policy on a broad array of foreign policy issues, ranging from Iraq, to Iran, to Al Qaeda. Having given over seven hundred briefings to high-level officials at the invitation of the White House, the State Department, the CIA, and the House of Representatives' International Relations Committee, as well as governments throughout Europe, Hulsman brings real-world experience to his analysis of what has gone wrong with American foreign policy, and how to put it right. As Anatol Lieven has done in the past, Hulsman is taking a professional risk in writing this book. One of the points of bonding for the two authors is that it is a risk that must be taken, if personal integrity is to be maintained and America put on a better foreign policy course.

Initially a supporter of the Iraq War, Hulsman served on both Heritage Foundation and Council on Foreign Relations task forces designed to provide Bush administration officials with policy advice for administering Iraq following the overthrow of Saddam Hussein. It was here that Hulsman started having doubts. First, it became clear the administration was not taking outside opinions seriously in terms of its Iraq strategy. Second, it was obvious that the Bush White House did not feel the need for much thinking on postwar reconstruction at all, as neoconservative ideological blinders led it to believe that there would be no significant political problems (let alone an insurgency), as Iraqis would welcome the American imposition of democracy. Third, when it became clear that things were not going as planned, the Bush administration responded with a curiously hollow admonition to "stay the course," rather than to look at what was going on in Iraq itself, and how problems could be fixed. As a result of these glaring intellectual errors, centered on an unforgivable moral hubris, the Iraq policy has descended into chaos.

Given these different backgrounds, our cooperation has not always been easy. In particular, Anatol Lieven comes from a far more statist tradition in social and economic terms, John Hulsman from a far more free market and even libertarian one. On various issues of domestic policy, we disagree considerably. And concerning global warming and the environment, while we are both deeply worried by what is happening, our proposed answers are so different that we have had to agree to differ, and so this issue, though vital, will have to be the subject of a different book.

On the other key foreign policy and security challenges facing the United States and its allies we are, however, at one. We share a common exasperation with the pieties and orthodoxies of both U.S. party establishments, and a common feeling that both are failing to provide answers—or rather, are providing the same wrong answers—to the grave challenges facing America and the rest of the West today. We share an anger that through a variety of different pressures, these party leaderships are seeking to enforce these orthodoxies on their followers. By doing so, they are depriving the American people of a genuine foreign policy debate, and a genuine foreign policy choice.

In terms of real differences, the party labels no longer mean much. There are many liberal hawks in the Democratic Party who are just as messianic in their ideology and aggressive in their basic attitudes to the outside world as are members of the Bush administration. They are opposed by Democratic "radicals" who resemble old-style conservative realists in calling for America to see the world through the eyes of other nations and learn to take their interests and views seriously.

On the other hand, large parts of the core Republican tradition are radically alienated from the policies of the current occupants of the White House. They are searching for a way back to the Republican tradition of President Dwight D. Eisenhower, and beyond him to the ideological and cultural roots of the Republican Party in the thinking of the Founders of the American republic.

We have therefore decided to turn our backs on the orthodoxy of both parties. Instead, we call on sensible and moderate people from both parties to work together to oppose the currently dominant mixture of ignorant utopianism and megalomaniacal ambition, a program that, if it is not stopped, will inevitably lead America to overreach itself, suffer defeat, and decline. Looking to the tenets of ethical realism, and to the historical examples of leaders like Harry S. Truman and Dwight Eisenhower, who applied those tenets in a bipartisan battle against Communism, we offer a new vision of foreign policy that will enable us to fight a stronger war against the enemies we face today, and, more important, create a decent international order for the future.

ANATOL LIEVEN AND JOHN HULSMAN,
Washington, D.C.,
April 2006

ETHICAL REALISM

One

LESSONS OF THE TRUMAN-EISENHOWER MOMENT

The best test of truth is the power of the thought to get itself accepted in the competition of the market.
—OLIVER WENDELL HOLMES

With the passing of George Kennan in March 2005, the last living member of the Truman administration, the most successful foreign policy team in modern American history, left the stage. Between 1945 and 1960, these men and their successors and de facto allies in the Eisenhower administration set the United States on the road to eventual victory in the Cold War. The success of the containment doctrine that they developed can be gauged by the fact that it was followed in one form or another until the collapse of the Soviet Union.

The triumph of the Truman years is all the more remarkable given that at the time of his swearing in, Harry Truman's only trip overseas had been as an artillery officer in World War I; he had never spoken to a Soviet citizen. What he did possess was native shrewdness; tremendous strength of character; deep patriotism and sense of responsibility; and not least, the self-confidence to appoint brilliant men to positions of responsibility and then back them to the hilt. For in the wake of World War II, with a new threat, Soviet Communism, facing the West, Truman and his team, somewhat unexpectedly followed by Eisenhower, established an entirely new model for American foreign policy that led to victory against an entirely different sort of enemy.

The threat of Soviet Communist expansionism after 1945 was not a sudden shock like Pearl Harbor or 9/11, but it was just as much of a jolt to the American system and attitudes. For the first time, the United States was faced with the need for permanent mobilization to meet a severe and open-ended global threat and maintain an indefinite and massive set of global commitments.

Until the Cold War, America's military commitments beyond its shores had always been brief, and with a predictable end. Most were short wars, after which it was assumed that America would go home; in the case of the occupations of the Philippines and several Caribbean nations after the defeat of Spain, the overseas commitments were small-scale. None of them required the United States to create a permanent conscript army or permanent security institutions like those the European states had had to develop over the centuries. Indeed, much of America's political tradition, since the first days of the colonies, was founded precisely on hostility to such "standing armies."

Not only did the Cold War now require such massive permanent mobilization, but the existence of atomic bombs made a general war with a relatively quick victory with limited losses—as in previous wars—difficult to imagine. After the United States and the Soviet Union both developed thermonuclear weapons, easy victory was almost impossible to imagine. The United States had to learn to live for the first time with permanent tension, which some found unbearable.

The war on terror is of course very different, but it is equally difficult to imagine any quick and successful end to it, especially through U.S. military action. Terrorism, like nuclear weapons, makes nonsense of General Douglas A. MacArthur's dictum that "in war there can be no substitute for victory." The substitute is holding the line and preventing the enemy from winning—which is what civilized states have been doing vis-à-vis barbarian enemies since the beginning of recorded time. The Byzantines never did "win" conclusively against their enemies, any more than successive Chinese dynasties did against their own barbarian menace. But

they held them off for centuries, during which time great civilizations flourished and eventually produced the societies and tech-
nologies by which the barbarian threat could be extinguished.

The Soviet threat therefore required a radical reconfiguration of
U.S. institutions and global strategy. Even more important, it
required a fundamental rethinking of America's vision of its role in
the world—"a complete revolution in American foreign policy and
the attitude of the American people," as Truman's secretary of state
Dean Acheson called it.[1] The old comforting nostrums of George
Washington's Farewell Address, of avoiding foreign entanglements
at all costs, made little sense in a world where ignoring Adolf
Hitler's rise had already led to such cataclysmic results. Ignoring
Soviet ambitions to dominate the world was simply no longer an
option. New thinking, based on these new realities, was vital.

The Truman administration, followed by that of Eisenhower,
recognized the radically new, different, and long-term nature of the
struggle, and developed radically new strategies, institutions, and
forces to wage it. The National Security Act of 1947, introduced
eighteen months after relations with the Soviet Union began their
radical downhill slide, created a range of new and vitally important
government institutions, including the National Security Council,
the Central Intelligence Agency, and the Air Force (previously a
branch of the U.S. Army). It also created strict and clear rules for
operating procedures and relations between them. The revelation
of the catastrophic danger of terrorism that occurred on September 11, 2001, demanded an equally new institutional and strategic
response from the Bush administration—but did not receive it.

The Truman-Eisenhower period is worth studying because it is
an example of radical reform in the midst of crisis, but also because
of who was proved to be right by history and who was proved to be
wrong. Those who have obviously been proved right were the
authors of a tough but restrained strategy of "containing" Soviet
expansionism, without launching or unduly risking war; and of
meanwhile undermining Communism through the force of the
West's democratic and free market example. This took longer than

many of them had hoped—but given that we won completely in the end, a few decades of mostly peaceful struggle were surely preferable to nuclear cataclysm.

By contrast, the "preventive war" and "rollback" schools of thought during the Cold War were proved wrong on just about everything. And a river of wrongness has flowed down from them to their neoconservative descendants of today, many of whose ideas derive directly from those of the hard-liners of the Truman and Eisenhower eras. Would you buy advice on your investments from a firm that has been wrong for sixty years?

For despite hard-liners on the right and appeasers on the left who attempted to derail the Truman-Eisenhower moment, the establishment achieved a fundamental and brilliantly successful rethinking of strategy: the containment doctrine that defined the Truman-Eisenhower moment signaled something entirely new for the United States and the world. Such is also our task today. The efforts of the Bush administration and the neoconservatives to push their agenda have come to predictable grief in Iraq and elsewhere. We must invent something new if we are to avoid the fate of confusion, decline, and ultimate defeat that continuing to pursue such a course is fated to hold. Fortunately, America's past, and especially the Truman-Eisenhower era, provide inspiration on how to proceed.

The Truman Record

The Truman administration is a tale of both what it did (the Marshall Plan and the creation of NATO) and what it did not do (turn the Korean War into a world war). Its guiding foreign policy strategy, the containment doctrine, was clearly laid down at the start, but also evolved over time, as events influenced the thinking of the administration.

Despite the evident hostility of Stalin's regime toward the West, abandoning the wartime alliance with the Soviet Union was not easy for the Truman administration. Although the U.S. establish-

ment and most ordinary Americans had always been deeply suspicious of Communism, the wartime alliance with the Soviet Union
had created real feelings of friendship, and even more important,
passionate hopes that long-term U.S.-Soviet cooperation would
ensure peace and progress for humanity in general.

Initially, therefore, it was not the Red Army's conquest of Eastern Europe in the final days of World War II that primarily
unnerved Washington. Rather, Moscow began to set its sights on
areas of clear strategic importance to the United States that lay
beyond the war's demarcation lines; in seeking to maintain its military presence in northern Iran in 1946 and in threatening Turkey's
sole control of the Dardanelles strait, it appeared that Moscow was,
like the Nazis, trying rapidly to dominate the world.

George Kennan, then acting head of the U.S. embassy in Moscow, proposed a different explanation of Soviet behavior. His "Long
Telegram" back to Washington is probably the single most important State Department cable ever written. For what Kennan did was
to give voice to the growing American unease about Soviet expansionism, give an explanation of what motivated this expansionism
and how it operated, and propound a strategy for dealing with it.
He laid the intellectual basis for the containment doctrine that was
eventually to bring the United States victory in the Cold War.

In an essay of 1947 based on the telegram, Kennan wrote,

> The first of the [Soviet Communist] concepts is that of the innate
> antagonism between capitalism and socialism. . . . It must invariably
> be assumed in Moscow that the aims of the capitalist worlds are
> antagonistic to the Soviet regime, and therefore to the interests of
> the peoples it controls. . . . And from [this belief in natural antago-
> nism] flow many of the phenomena which we find disturbing in
> the Kremlin's conduct of foreign policy: the secretiveness, the lack
> of frankness, the duplicity, the wary suspiciousness and the basic
> unfriendliness of purpose.[2]

Today, this portrayal seems self-evident, denied only by a few elements of the old left. It is difficult to exaggerate, however, its star-

tling and essential effect on Americans of early 1946, and especially liberals, passionately anxious to believe that the Soviet Union, which had made such terrible sacrifices in the struggle against Nazism, and "good old Uncle Joe" Stalin himself, were basically decent, and wanted good relations with the United States.

Kennan saw Stalin and the Soviet Communists as essentially expansionist, but also cautious, because they saw history as on their side and therefore could afford to wait. Compared with the Nazis, they were more rational, and would not force the pace in their drive for global dominance. The Soviet leadership therefore proceeded not according to some strategic doctrine, but opportunistically. They would constantly probe for political, social, and economic weaknesses and divisions in the non-Communist world, seeking to exploit these to their benefit. Unlike the Nazis, however, they would also stop or retreat wherever they met strong resistance, rather than driving ahead, ignoring the risks and the cost. There was rarely a need for America to adopt "threats or blustering or superfluous gestures of outward 'toughness.' " Instead, Kennan said,

> It is a sine qua non of successful dealing with Russia that the government in question should remain at all times cool and collected and that its demands on Russian policy should be put forward in such a manner as to leave the way open for a compliance not too detrimental to Russian prestige.

Kennan recommended that Washington adopt two broad strategic countermeasures. First, the containment doctrine drew demarcation lines between the non-Communist and Communist worlds, with the American priority going to bolster allies nearest the lines, such as West Germany, Iran, Greece, Turkey, Japan, and later, South Korea. Second, it would be critically important to build up the free world economically and socially, as Communism thrived on economic suffering, social conflict, and political chaos.[3]

The Korean War is the classic example of the military aspects of containment being put to the test, with the United States and its allies—after stumbling very badly twice in the first six months of the war—ultimately defeating North Korean dictator Kim Il Sung's dreams of a unified Communist Korea. It was preceded by U.S. and British measures to strengthen militarily the anti-Communist side in Greece's civil war. The Marshall Plan, Truman's grand effort to stabilize Western Europe, is the great expression of the equally critical nonmilitary aspects of the doctrine.[4] This simple, carefully limited strategy was crowned by the fact that the Soviet Union ultimately committed suicide, much as Kennan had predicted with almost uncanny accuracy forty-five years before:

> [Unless its Communist economy radically changes] Russia will remain economically a vulnerable and in some sense an impotent nation. . . . Soviet power is only a crust concealing an amorphous mass of human beings among whom no independent organizational structure is tolerated. . . . If, consequently, anything were ever to occur to disrupt the unity and efficacy of the Party as a political instrument, Soviet Russia might be changed overnight from one of the strongest to one of the weakest and most pitiable of national societies.

Rarely in history has such analytical brilliance led to such wise policy recommendations being followed over such a long period of time. Critical to this success was not only the wisdom of the policy itself, but the creation of bipartisan domestic consensus that—in the face of heavy odds—ensured that Truman's strategy was followed by Eisenhower's Republican administration.

Harry Truman succeeded in politically isolating the left wing of the Democratic Party, which favored some sort of accommodation with the U.S.S.R. (epitomized by former vice president and 1948 presidential candidate Henry Wallace). The hard-line, preventive war wing of the Republican Party, symbolized by General Douglas MacArthur, was likewise marginalized.

Instead of either accommodation or war, political competition with the Soviets became the modus operandi in the immediate post-1945 era. This state of affairs was reinforced by the election of Dwight Eisenhower in 1952, a Republican who essentially continued his Democratic predecessor's strategy. In seeing off these threats to a bipartisan foreign policy, the Truman and Eisenhower administrations laid the basis for eventual victory in the Cold War.

The "Truman-Eisenhower moment" was also a "Churchill-Bevin moment," when tough-minded members of Britain's Labour government—including moderate socialists—joined with the Conservative opposition to create a new alliance with the United States to resist Soviet expansionism.[5] This contributed in turn to the rallying of both Christian Democrat and Social Democrat leaders across Western Europe to the same cause. None of this could have been achieved if the United States during that period had pursued a strategy of reckless ideological unilateralism.

Such unilateralism has been characteristic of today's neoconservatives, and the Bush administration, and has created immense problems for U.S. strategy. For unilateralism can so easily become a self-fulfilling prophecy, leading to an America that cannot find allies even if it later seeks them. As the history of America and Europe in the early years of the Cold War makes clear, courting allies does not show weakness—it is a requirement of strategic success in a world where the United States is preeminent but not all-powerful, and is facing powerful enemies and intractable challenges.

The Truman-Eisenhower continuity did not stem from personal affinity between the two men; Truman never forgave Eisenhower for not defending General Marshall from the vile and unfounded attacks of Senator Joseph McCarthy. Nor did Eisenhower ever ask his predecessor for advice the way Truman had consulted former president Herbert Hoover. Well into his retirement, Truman could hardly say anything about Eisenhower without resorting to profanity.[6]

What mattered above all was that the majority of men in each administration rejected both "the yahoos of the right and the softies of the left."[7] Both Truman and Eisenhower favored political competition with the Soviet Union whenever possible, spurning both Wallace's siren call that there need not be such a competition at all, and General MacArthur's pleas for a preventive military Armageddon.

The two basic reasons that containment doctrine proved so successful in the political marketplace are that it was quickly seen to work by most sensible observers and that it enjoyed bipartisan support. With the Marshall Plan restoring Western Europe's economic and political stability, the Soviet Union had fewer and fewer chances to seek advantage. Likewise by showing that aggression did not pay in Korea, the United States gave smaller countries around the world more confidence that it would defend them.

But even more than quick policy success, the bipartisan nature of the support for containment allowed the policy to survive immediate changes in political fortunes, becoming the majority strategic view of both political parties, thus acquiring permanence rarely seen in American politics. Both Truman and Eisenhower achieved this bipartisan consensus through convincing leading opponents of the superiority of the containment strategy—not, as too often under Bush, through seeking to intimidate them into submission with accusations of a lack of patriotism.

If America is to find solid footing for continued leadership in this new era of the war on terror, the Truman-Eisenhower example must be examined in greater detail.

Building Up Western Europe: The Genius of the Marshall Plan

By 1947 it was clear that Western Europe was in both economic and political danger of leaving the American orbit; uncertainty and chaos were serving Soviet interests. In France and Italy, Communist parties loyal to Stalin were emerging as the strongest single political units. The Truman administration then rallied the U.S.

establishment around a daring initiative to save Western Europe from Communism—the Marshall Plan. If chaos in Western Europe was the friend of Moscow, prosperity and the stability that flowed from it would drastically limit the potential for Communist revolution and Soviet adventurism. Eventually, in the vision of the plan's creators, the evident superiority of the Western model would also undermine Communism within the Soviet bloc itself.

The plan, as outlined by Secretary of State Marshall, and developed in detail by then under secretary of state Dean Acheson, had two parts. First, the idea was to allow Europeans to help themselves. While America was to put up a then unheard-of $16 billion, it was the Europeans who were to work out the details, thereby making them stakeholders in the process; America therefore was to supply the means but not dictate the results. Only by being able to count on a firm alliance with Great Britain was Washington able to make the Marshall Plan work, for it was London that then took the lead organizing like-minded continental allies. A greater contrast to the Bush administration's initially centralized and unilateral efforts to reconstruct Iraq can hardly be imagined.

While the fact that Winston Churchill, then leader of the Conservative opposition and a lifelong anti-Communist, supported Washington's plans was in itself unremarkable, his critically important alliance with the moderate socialist foreign secretary of the ruling Labour Party was on the face of it far more unlikely. Ernest Bevin was the short and squat illegitimate son of a barmaid. He was also well read, blunt, determined, and intelligent. As a social democrat, he had been fighting against Communist infiltration of the Labour Party and British trade union politics for most of his life.[8] Following Labour's smashing victory in the 1945 elections, Bevin found himself foreign secretary. While Prime Minister Clement Attlee concentrated on the domestic reforms that were to establish the modern British welfare system, Bevin was left with great autonomy to conduct foreign policy.

Acheson was right to target Bevin, who immediately grasped the significance of Marshall's speech. As he listened to Marshall over the BBC, Bevin later said, he felt that the Marshall Plan was "like a lifeline to a sinking man."9 He wasted no time, immediately cabling the State Department that he intended to go to Paris to coordinate planning with the other European leaders. When Bevin was forced by illness to resign in March 1950, Churchill lauded him, saying in a March 17 party political broadcast that Bevin had strengthened Britain's ties with America, while exhibiting "his steadfast resistance to communist aggression."10

Yet even with wholehearted British support, establishing the European plans for Marshall money was not easy. Truman dispatched Averell Harriman, his diplomatic jack-of-all-trades, to be the American coordinator for Marshall aid. Harriman was at his best, finessing outcomes without ever dictating results. For example, he managed to overcome still strong French resistance to helping West Germany, as Paris for obvious reasons then preferred to keep it weak. Harriman overcame all such obstacles; the Marshall Plan came in at cost.

The second plank of the plan was even more risky: the Soviets were not to be excluded from Marshall aïd. Kennan felt particularly strongly that America must not be blamed for the coming division in Europe that the Marshall Plan was helping to cement. The gamble paid off. The Soviets refused to take part in further European discussions about Marshall aid, as they would not allow an accounting of how they intended to spend the money. Further, they forbade their East European satellites, desperate for Marshall funds, from participating in the program.

When this Soviet strategy failed to blunt the Marshall Plan, Stalin used his control of Western European Communist parties to launch general strikes in France and Italy. Such tactics alienated many, with the strikes signaling the last hurrah of Stalinism in Western Europe. By building up Western Europe, Truman's men had succeeded in politically winning the battle for influence there. As President Truman put it, when asked the reasoning behind the Marshall Plan, "I am doing it because it is right, I am doing it because it is necessary to be done if we are going to survive ourselves."11

The Marshall Plan was an embodiment in action of the principles of ethical realism, which we will put forward in chapter three.
It was deeply moral, generous, and enlightened, but it also met all
the traditional standards of realism. It was clearly in the national
interests of the United States—even though many Americans did
not recognize this at the time. It had its tough, even sneaky aspect,
in the way that it trapped the Soviet regime diplomatically. And
given the risks involved, it required great moral courage in its
creators. Reinhold Niebuhr described it as the epitome of ethical
realism in action. It is this combination of the idealistic and the
practical that has so often characterized American foreign policy at
its best: a mixture worth rediscovering today.

Politically, the best thing the administration had going for it was
that the plan was named after Marshall, rather than the unpopular
president. As Truman quipped, "Anything that is sent up to the
Senate or the House with my name on it will quiver a couple of
times and die."[12] Far better to make General Marshall, who was
often compared to George Washington, the focal point of the program. He was a figure of flawless rectitude, with an ironclad sense
of duty. Because of his role as Army chief of staff in creating the
military economy and the forces that won the Second World War
for the United States, he was loved both by Truman and by congressional Republicans. Marshall's unique status made him the
perfect choice to advocate on behalf of the plan that bears his name.

And Marshall put the case to Congress in apocalyptic terms. He
warned that if America decided it was "unable or unwilling effectively to assist in the reconstruction of Western Europe, we must
accept the consequences of its collapse into the dictatorship of
police states . . . there is no doubt in my mind that the whole world
hangs in the balance."[13] Given the source of the comments, it was
almost impossible for congressional Republicans to say no to such
a plea. With the Communist coup in Czechoslovakia and the advent
of the Berlin crisis, even sworn foes of the administration such as
Senator Robert Taft ended up voting for the plan.

Defeating Henry Wallace and the Threat from the Left

In order to establish containment as the guiding doctrine of U.S. strategy, Truman had to defeat threats from both the left and the right. The first of these came from the left wing of his own Democratic Party, led by his commerce secretary, Henry Wallace. For many Democrats, Wallace was the rightful heir to Franklin Roosevelt. Having served as vice president throughout Roosevelt's third term, Wallace was a far better known figure nationally than the newly sworn-in Harry Truman, who had never been personally close to FDR. The dramatic manner in which Truman assumed the presidency made it vital that he be seen as the clear heir to the fallen leader; Wallace's differing perspective on the Cold War and mere political existence made him a constant threat to Truman.

From the start, Wallace opposed containment on the grounds that it was based on an exaggerated estimate of Soviet expansionism, and that it was U.S. policies, rather than Soviet ones, that were primarily responsible for worsening tensions, dividing the world, and risking new war. While continuing to serve in Truman's cabinet, Wallace told a gathering of his supporters at Madison Square Garden, on September 12, 1946, that the American alliance with Britain needlessly threatened the Soviet Union. He said that a spheres-of-influence foreign policy should mean America did not care what Stalin was doing in Eastern Europe, as long as the Soviet Union did not promote Communist revolution in Western Europe or Latin America. He indirectly criticized Truman's far tougher line with the Soviets, saying, "The tougher we get the tougher the Russians will get."[14] For Wallace, containment doctrine was making the Cold War into a self-fulfilling prophecy.

When Truman confronted Wallace and fired him, the latter's support in the country at large turned out in the end to be small. However, within the ranks of Democratic Party activists his popularity was much greater. Young liberals, some blue-collar workers, blacks, and socialists (including some Communists) supported him. It seemed for a while that this would be enough to bring very serious pressure to bear on Truman, and force him either to change his policy or to lose the 1948 election to his Republican rival, Thomas Dewey, as a result of Wallace's third-party candidacy.

The majority of the decision-makers within the Truman administration wholly repudiated such talk as Wallace's. George Kennan warned that the concessions to Moscow demanded by Wallace would lead to "unabashed demands for further concessions at every point."[15] Memories of where the appeasement of Hitler had led naturally meant that such views had great resonance with the American public.

Furthermore, though Wallace was himself a deeply honorable patriot, he did seem to have a blind spot when it came to Stalin's well-known villainy. Although the extent of Stalin's purges in the 1930s was not then fully known, it was already irrefutable that millions of people had suffered and died under the Soviet despot. To assume benign motivations on Stalin's part, while at the same time skeptically questioning all of America's motives, seemed at once morally obtuse and politically woolly-headed.

Wallace campaigned for president in 1948 on a platform of turning American nuclear weapons over to the United Nations, and advocated funding a massive reconstruction program for the U.S.S.R. He was against the Marshall Plan, as he felt, with some justification, that it further divided the world in two. During the Berlin crisis, Wallace advocated giving West Berlin to the Soviets, saying the city was not worth a third world war. Wallace tried to unite the American left and the Democratic Party around a policy of fostering "one world," by engaging Stalin in direct negotiations to reach compromises and end the budding Cold War.

But Truman always had Wallace's number. During the 1948 campaign, he shrewdly portrayed his former colleague as naive and morally confused, rather than accusing him of treason. Truman charged the Communists with "guiding it and using it [the Wallace challenge]," and said "the third party did not represent American ideals."[16] In 1948, Truman decisively dealt with the threat to containment from the left; he won 28 states and 303 electoral votes, while Wallace won 1.1 million votes and no states. Until the Vietnam War split America, the left was never again to pose a serious threat to containment. Indeed, by far the strongest and most dangerous opposition to the creation of NATO and other key elements of containment strategy came from the right of the Republican Party.

Wallace's campaign exposed a fundamental lack of balance in his and the left's worldview. For example, during his acceptance speech for the new party's nomination, Wallace blamed American policy for the majority of the world's problems and tensions, while never once criticizing either Stalin or the Soviet Union.[17]

The greatest flaw in Wallace's thinking was that there was never a chance for bipartisan support for such a policy; no faction of the Republican Party would ever accept appeasement of Stalin. As such, Wallace's dreams of ending the Cold War were always likely to come to nothing, as all it would take to overturn such policies was an eventual Republican presidential victory. Running for president on a policy platform exaggeratedly critical of your own country is not likely to be popular in the United States or any other nation. But although the failure of the Wallace candidacy ended the threat to Truman from the left, a more dangerous enemy of containment, the far right of the Republican Party, was rising to oppose the president over the Korean crisis.

Korea: Checking Aggression While Avoiding World War

If the Marshall Plan was the Truman administration at its most proactive, the Korean War exemplified the masterful restraint shown by both Truman and then Eisenhower. It is in their adoption of the same Korean policy, beyond all else, that the Truman-Eisenhower continuity was forged.

Margaret Truman, the president's daughter, records what the stakes were in Korea. "My father made it clear from the moment he heard the news, that he feared this was the opening of World War III."[18] It was assumed in America that Stalin, through his control of international Communism, was directing Kim Il Sung's attack on the South Korean regime of Syngman Rhee from Moscow. We now know the truth was more complicated than this; while Stalin knew of and approved the attack, hoping America would consider Korea outside its containment perimeter, the initiator of the attack was Kim Il Sung himself, for essentially Korean reasons. Nonetheless, the Truman administration was correct to assume that if the North Korean Communists had been allowed to get away with the conquest of the South, it would probably have emboldened Moscow to support or conduct aggressive action elsewhere.

Truman reacted quickly and decisively. His administration's strategy was based on two principles: America must not ignore the aggression from the North, as its failure to act would discredit American leadership throughout the world. At the same time the conflict must be kept within bounds, to avoid the potential for a world war.

In August 1950, Truman sent Averell Harriman with a message to General Douglas MacArthur: "Tell him two things. One, I'm going to do everything I can to give him what he wants in the way of support; and secondly, I want you to tell him I do not want to get into a war with the Chinese communists."[19] This was the advent of the doctrine of limited war—that clashes between the American-led and Communist worlds must be restrained in the short run, giving time for containment to work in the long run. It was not going to be an easy sell to the American people, with their historical tradition of complete victory.

After MacArthur's brilliant counterattack at Inchon, the United States became intoxicated with victory. American objectives in Korea, up until then clearly limited by the administration, became more ambitious. With everyone from right-wing senators to *The New York Times* in agreement, the object was broadened to include the destruction of the North Korean forces and the unification of the peninsula under American and U.N. protection. For the first time, the immediate rollback of Communism, and not just its containment, seemed a real strategic possibility. In fact, the following months were to illustrate the catastrophic dangers of such a course.

Even while expanding the mission, Truman made clear to the victorious general that his caveats about not fighting the Chinese still applied. MacArthur was allowed to go north of the 38th parallel dividing North and South Korea only if there was no sign of Chinese or Soviet intervention; he was also to keep a certain distance from the North Korean–Chinese border to avoid provocation.

Yet when U.S. forces on MacArthur's orders in fact moved ever northward, American diplomats ignored Chinese foreign minister Chou En-lai's warnings that the situation was intolerable for Peking and that it would intervene to save its North Korean fellow Communists. In November 1950, the Chinese attacked with 300,000 men, driving U.S. forces southward in what for a time seemed to be a hopeless rout that would end with the evacuation of the entire peninsula and a defeat that would undermine American prestige and leadership across the world.

In response, MacArthur urged that between thirty and fifty atom bombs be dropped on Chinese Manchuria. Yet despite the intense pressure, the Truman administration stuck to its line that the war must not be expanded. The intense risk of nuclear war only lasted a few weeks, until the new commander on the ground, General Matthew Ridgway, rallied the U.S. and allied troops and stopped the Chinese and North Korean advance—but they were crucial weeks for the future and even the survival of mankind.

MacArthur was outraged by the Truman administration's restraint, feeling that Washington was crippling his efforts to defeat international Communism in Korea. And indeed, in advocating a limited war in Korea, the Truman administration was promoting a whole new way to think strategically, one that was both foreign and odious to those, like the general, who had been schooled in the all-or-nothing certainties of World War II.

Influenced by his Korean obsession and the growing peril to his own reputation, MacArthur thought only of immediate tactics, and not of the larger international concerns Truman was trying to balance with what was happening on the Korean peninsula. The primary political goal, in line with containment, was once again to turn back the North Korean aggression and restore the 38th parallel as the demarcation line between North and South, not to widen the war to try to crush the Chinese Communists, with all the perils of that course.

Tension between MacArthur and the administration reached a climax on March 24, 1951, when, without consulting the White House, MacArthur declared publicly that the Chinese should take care to no longer count on American restraint. He mentioned the possibility of expanding the war by striking at China itself, presumably through air attacks and with nuclear weapons.

Truman was furious. MacArthur compounded his disregard of the basic constitutional principle that civilians, and not the military, set overall policy in America by secretly corresponding with House Minority Leader Joe Martin, a leading critic of the administration. When Martin made public the general's reservations about the administration, Truman finally fired MacArthur on April 11, 1951. As the historian David McCullough writes, "Nothing had so stirred the political passions since the Civil War"[20] as Truman's firing of MacArthur. For many in America, particularly those involved in the Pacific theater, MacArthur was the primary hero of the Second World War.

For Truman the firing of MacArthur could not have come at a worse time. A Gallup poll showed Truman's approval rating at the time of the firing at 26 percent, his then all-time low. According to the same pollster, fully 69 percent of the country was with MacArthur at the time of his dismissal. Of 44,358 telegrams received by Republicans in Congress in the first forty-eight hours after the firing, all but 334 sided with MacArthur.[21] Seven and a half million people attended his welcome in New York by ticker-tape parade. This reception made clear just how easy it would have been, under different, less wise, and less resolute political leadership, for the

United States to have plunged into a new world war with the broad support of the political class and most ordinary Americans.

A record 30 million people watched the returning hero speak before Congress. MacArthur continued to insist that "there is no substitute for victory." His view, as earlier expressed to Harriman, was, "We should fight the Communists everywhere—fight them like hell!"[22] MacArthur's attitude, which acknowledged no limits on American power and no distinction between the different Communist states and movements, was an invitation to an unlimited conflict with both China and the Soviet Union; World War III, with each side possessing nuclear weapons, could not be far away. This inability to set priorities in certain areas (and thus limits in others) is what plagues neoconservatives and their Democratic hawk allies today. History makes it clear that such a vision leads to overstretching and decline.

While a masterful oration, MacArthur's swift demise can be dated from the speech. For in it he wrongly claimed that the Joint Chiefs, who had actually strongly opposed his efforts to widen the war in Korea, shared his views. By playing fast and loose with the truth, MacArthur discredited himself, and in the process, his views on the rollback of Communism as well. When the Joint Chiefs publicly refuted him, his support rapidly ebbed.[23]

Eisenhower as Truman's Heir

In the presidential election of 1952, Eisenhower won the largest popular vote since FDR in 1936, gaining 442 electoral votes to a mere 89 for Governor Adlai Stevenson of Illinois. Clearly 1952 was an Eisenhower, rather than a Republican, triumph. While squeaking through to narrow majorities in both the House and the Senate, across the country the party ran far behind the hero of Normandy. This political reality was to prove crucial, for it gave Eisenhower the leeway to support Truman's containment policy in the face of fierce criticism from segments of his own party.

During and immediately after the election campaign, it seemed that the Eisenhower White House would develop a very different foreign policy strategy from that of Truman. The 1952 Republican foreign policy platform, written by John Foster Dulles (soon to be secretary of state), vowed that Republican victory "will mark the end of the negative, futile and immoral policy of 'containment' which abandons human beings to despotism and Godless Communism."[24]

Eisenhower publicly—though not necessarily sincerely—affirmed his support for the Dulles position. Speaking to the American Legion on August 24, 1952, he said that the United States should use its "influence and power" to help the satellite nations of Eastern Europe throw off the "yoke of Russian tyranny."[25] But once in office Eisenhower quickly began to adopt Truman's policies. He made it clear to Dulles, then a strong advocate of a rollback of Soviet power, that he had to add the words "all peaceful means" whenever publicly discussing the liberation of the captive peoples of Prague, Budapest, or Warsaw.

In the face of a Korean War mired for more than two years in stalemate at the 38th parallel, Eisenhower also soon realized that a peaceful outcome would require acceptance of the concept of limited war—though this was hated by advocates of rollback in general, and the old guard of his own party in particular.

Eisenhower's affirmation of Truman's Korea policy therefore took some of the same qualities of steel that Truman had shown in confronting MacArthur, and that Eisenhower had shown in his leadership during the Second World War. He had to face down Dr. Syngman Rhee, strongman of South Korea; his own secretary of state, Dulles; and General Mark Clark, commander of U.N. forces in Korea since 1952—all of whom called for a policy of rollback. When the Korean armistice talks stalled, Eisenhower made it clear that a nuclear strike could not be ruled out if they broke down—but as Kennan had advised in such cases, he did so privately, so as not to risk forcing the North Korean regime and its backers into a tough response.

The agreement was finally signed six months into his term—

leaving North Korea firmly in Communist hands, which was not at all what most of the Republican Party had wanted. Three circumstances allowed Eisenhower to flout the rollback platform on which he had been elected to the presidency: his skill at political-bureaucratic maneuver, his phenomenal personal popularity, and the popularity of an end to the war. As Eisenhower's biographer Stephen Ambrose notes,

> His [Eisenhower's] solution was acceptable only because he had put his own immense prestige behind it; he knew that if Truman had agreed to such a settlement, Republican fury might have led to an impeachment attempt and certainly would have had a divisive effect on the country.[26]

The political irony was apparent. In Korea, Truman could not carry out his policy of seeking peace. Only the head of the opposing party could do so. This was the beginning of the political bipartisan support for containment, later favored by Democrats such as John F. Kennedy and Lyndon Johnson, and Republicans such as Richard Nixon, a state of affairs that gave the doctrine the time it needed to make its predictions of Communism's demise eventually come to pass.

However, in the mid-1950s the temptation to engage in preventive war remained very strong—even on occasions for Truman and Eisenhower themselves. This was because of the huge, but inevitably temporary, lead the United States possessed over the U.S.S.R. in thermonuclear weapons. Added to this was the fear that once the Soviets achieved parity they would use this to launch a conventional attack, reckoning that the United States would not dare risk annihilation by escalating to nuclear warfare.

As General Orvil Anderson, commander of the Air War College, told his officers, "Give me the order to do it, and I can break up Russia's five A-bomb nests in a week. . . . And when I went up to Christ—I think that I could explain to Him that I had saved civilization."[27] This is a dilemma that America faces again today, in a lesser form, when it debates whether to launch strikes intended to prevent—or rather most probably only delay—Iran from gaining nuclear weapons.

Eisenhower defeated the preventive war and rollback arguments within his new administration partly through a brilliant maneuver in the summer of 1953 called the "Solarium Exercise," after the room in the White House where it took place. Eisenhower ordered the formation of three teams, each of which was to argue for a different U.S. strategy in dealing with the Soviet Union: Team C argued for a full attempt at rollback, even at a high risk of nuclear war; Team B argued for a milder but still aggressive strategy of undermining Communist rule in China and the Soviet satellites; and Team A called for a continuation of containment.

Ostensibly, Solarium was set up as a level playing field. However, Eisenhower indicated his own preferences when he picked George Kennan to lead Team A and praised him highly in his introductory remarks. This was striking enough, given that Kennan had been unceremoniously fired from the State Department by Dulles only a few weeks before, and given that Kennan had already issued a number of statements complaining that his successors (like Paul Nitze) had greatly overemphasized the military aspects of his containment strategy at the expense of the economic, political, and diplomatic ones.

While the president claimed diplomatically that Solarium had demonstrated that there were in fact considerable underlying similarities between the positions of the three teams, the real effect of the exercise was to force the senior ranks of the bureaucracy and military to think through in detail the implications of rollback and preventive war, and realize that they were either unworkable or not worth the high risk of nuclear holocaust. The result was the National Security Council document number 162, which continued the containment strategy virtually unchanged.[28]

During the discussions on the teams' conclusions, Eisenhower, in Kennan's view, "showed his intellectual ascendancy over every man in the room." In particular, Eisenhower expressed two critically important perceptions that too many of the other participants had missed. First, he asked, "What would we do with Russia, if we should win a global war? . . . The colossal job of occupying the territories of the defeated enemy would be far beyond the resources of the United States at the end of such a war."[29] This is a question that the George H. W. Bush administration asked itself about Iraq in 1990–91—and that his son's administration completely failed to ask in 2002–03.

Second, Eisenhower fully realized that even victory in such a war would imperil America's own democratic system and traditions: "The only thing worse than losing a global war was winning one . . . there would be no individual freedom after the next global war." In his own notes, which American policymakers of today should learn by heart, Eisenhower wrote: "Global war as a defense of freedom: Almost contradiction in terms."[30] In this he directly echoed Truman's thinking.

Eisenhower's concern went beyond war itself to the effects on the United States of permanent mobilization for war. Throughout his presidency, he was deeply worried about the nation becoming what he called a "garrison state," like those of Europe in the past: a state that would militarize American society and culture, suppress American freedoms, and seek out unnecessary conflicts. The fact that a famous general should have been so intelligently suspicious of security institutions, practices, and motives is a tribute to Eisenhower's greatness as a man, but also to the greatness of the civic tradition that produced him. He was indeed, as he himself said of Churchill, "a soldier, statesman and *citizen*" (Eisenhower's emphasis).[31]

Unfortunately, and despite all of Truman's and Eisenhower's warnings, the decades of the Cold War have produced Americans too accustomed to a security state, and a dominant national security elite that their ancestors would have found monstrous; indeed, American students of today, when asked who first warned against the power of the U.S. "military-industrial complex," are all too likely to reply, "Wasn't it some Communist?"

Eisenhower also instinctively understood, as had Truman and his key officials, the vital nonmilitary aspects of containment and of national strength. The defense budget had increased 300 percent during the last two and a half years of the Truman administration; Eisenhower wanted it cut. As he told a frustrated Dulles, "Our defense depends on our fiscal system."[32] Reflecting the president's views, his national security adviser, Robert Cutler, declared that the argument for hugely expanding the military to support a rollback strategy "entirely fails to recognize that the threat to our economy and liberty [from overspending and prolonged deficits] is co-equal to the threat from external aggression."[33]

This meant balancing the budget; and the government ended fiscal 1960 with a $1 billion surplus, despite the pressures to continually increase defense spending. Eisenhower, like Kennan, was proved right; when the Soviet empire did implode, it was as much due to its relative economic shortcomings as to anything else. Eisenhower, as have so few in Washington over the past half century, saw the direct link between overall security and fiscal responsibility. This is a lesson that has surely eluded the Bush administration and the neoconservatives of our own time.

Truman and Eisenhower were both worried about a growing national debt that would be owned by Americans and Europeans. What on earth would they have had to say about a situation in which a Republican administration has allowed the current account deficit to make America a possible hostage not to its friends but to rivals and even potential enemies, like China? Or about the incredible waste and corruption that has attended U.S. spending within Iraq, and that has helped make fleeting budget surpluses into monstrous deficits?

Eisenhower referred repeatedly to the fact that the strength of a nation lies ultimately not in arms but in its ability to provide decently for its people. Soon after he took office, in a speech entitled "The Chance for Peace," he listed all the schools and hospitals that the United States could build for its people for the cost of one bomber, and declared, "This is not a way of life at all, in any true sense. Under the cloud of threatening war, it is humanity hanging from a cross of iron."[34]

Eisenhower understood that "moral authority" was not just a phrase for the weak; world opinion matters a great deal to American power. As he made clear in an unpublished portion of his memoirs, regarding possible American intervention in Vietnam, "The standing of the United States as the most powerful of the anticolonial powers is an asset of incalculable value to the Free World. . . . The moral position of the United States was more to be guarded than the Tonkin Delta, indeed than all of Indochina."[35]

The former supreme commander of the Allied forces in Europe during World War II also knew—as few civilian politicians could and as the neoconservatives and the Bush administration certainly do not—the human costs of war. In 1954 alone, Eisenhower five times rebuffed calls from the foreign and defense policy establishment for U.S. military intervention in Asia. He explained that he had personally experienced "the job of writing letters of condolence by the hundreds, by the thousands, to bereaved mothers and wives. This is a very sobering experience."[36] He went on to say, in a declaration today's neoconservatives should study again and again, "Don't go to war in response to emotions of anger and resentment; do it prayerfully."[37]

In recognizing fiscal restraints, the importance of global moral standing, the threat of the "garrison state" to American liberties, the agonizing loss that war would bring, and the probable futility of military "victory," Eisenhower was predisposed to adopt a policy that had marked limits but left America in a position of preeminence. This certainly did not mean that a defeatist do-nothingism crept into his thinking. Rather, by making such choices, Eisenhower clearly saw that containment met his priorities, and would ultimately defeat the Soviet Union, while not undermining America itself.

The great majority of the American political system had come to a consensus. As a result, as Truman had declared in his valedictory speech of January 15, 1953, and in words that were later to be echoed by Eisenhower,

> When history says that my time of office saw the beginning of the Cold War, it will also say that in those eight years we have set the course that can win it. . . . As the free world grows stronger, more united, more attractive to men on both sides of the Iron Curtain— and as the Soviet hopes for easy expansion are blocked—then there will have to come a time of change in the Soviet world.[38]

Then and Now

Whereas Eisenhower and Truman created a brilliant new strategy for a new threat, the Bush administration reacted to 9/11 according to strategies and ways of looking at the world that were developed during the struggle with the Soviet Union. They were successful then, but are largely irrelevant to the conflict with Islamist extremism and terrorism. Thus in the wake of 9/11, it should have been blindingly obvious that by far the single most important security institution in the United States today is the human intelligence arm (HUMINT) of the CIA. Instead of prioritizing that arm, the Bush administration reacted in a way reminiscent of Cold War approaches at their worst: First it buried the CIA under a thick new layer of bureaucracy, and then it politicized that bureaucracy.[39] The record as regards domestic security is little better.

The United States is a great modern democracy, with fine institutions staffed by skilled, dedicated, and patriotic men and women. Nowhere is this more true than of America's security services. How then can it possibly be that when in December 2005 the bipartisan 9/11 Commission gave its verdict on the Bush administration's performance in carrying out the urgently necessary improvements in security against terrorism that it had recommended, it gave the administration five Fs, twelve Ds, eight Cs, and only one A—. This was seventeen months after it had made these urgent recommendations, and fifty-one months after 9/11. Even in the area of airline security—airline security, for God's sake!—the commission allotted an F, a C−, a C, and a D. We believe that Truman and Eisenhower would both have called this criminal negligence on the part of their successor.[40]

The Department of Homeland Security is widely described by insiders as a bureaucratic nightmare. The result has been confusion, savage infighting over turf, the crushing of individual talent in the lower ranks, intense and dangerous demoralization, and the loss of experienced and critically important staff. This has also ensured that the U.S. government is presented not with the truth from its agents, but only what it wants to hear.[41] Meanwhile, the administration has been spending colossal sums on Cold War–style weapons systems that are virtually irrelevant to the fight against terrorists.

In fact, while constantly using the language of war, the Bush administration has not behaved as if America is really at war. Whenever in the past America has been at war, U.S. administrations have done two things, both of which took moral courage: They have asked the American people—the elites as well as the mass of the population—for real sacrifices to support the war effort; and they have made hard choices in foreign policy, so as to be able to concentrate attention and resources on the chief enemy.

During the Second World War, the Roosevelt administration recognized that in order to defeat Germany it needed to give real support to the Soviet armies, which until June 1944 were doing by far the greater part of the fighting against Germany. During the Korean War, the Truman administration recognized that to contain Communism it would have to form alliances with some states and regimes of which it had previously been very suspicious. And when President Nixon and his secretary of state, Henry Kissinger, saw that America was going to have to abandon Vietnam, they drew the logical conclusion, and in defiance of much of their own party, forged a form of alliance with Communist China so as to contain Soviet and Vietnamese Communist expansionism. The Bush administration has failed in both these duties. It has failed to ask the American people to pay higher taxes or cut spending programs, leading to a budget deficit the scale of which is itself a threat to national security.

Even more seriously, the Bush administration, the neoconservatives and liberal hawks, most of Congress, and many leaders of the Democratic Party have failed in their duty to concentrate on the threat from Islamist extremism. The Bush administration, with Democrat acquiescence, initiated a failed war in Iraq that has allowed the Islamist terrorists to launch a new front against us, and that has gravely undermined our ability to intervene or even threaten anywhere else.

And even after this terrible lesson, the administration and the leaderships of both main parties continue to threaten Iran (despite that country's bitter hostility to Al Qaeda, the Taliban, and the Baath, the ruling party of Saddam Hussein); to try to roll back Russian influence in the former Soviet Union (although Russia too has been the target of frightful terrorist attacks); to put economic and strategic pressure on China; and to seek to isolate and even overthrow Venezuela's Hugo Chávez and other anti-American populists in Latin America. In isolation, each of these strategies may have something to be said for it. Put together, they are far beyond America's real strength. They represent strategic overstretch of a truly dangerous kind, risking defeat and humiliation in one or even all of these areas.

This partly reflects the fact that the administration, and much of the contemporary establishment in general, are obsessed with states rather than terrorists. In addition, too many have continued to view either Russia or China as America's primary rivals and enemies, instead of concentrating on the threat from Al Qaeda to modern states and modern civilization in general. This is a bit like the desire of Henry Wallace and the American left (and some of the right) after 1945 to ignore Soviet aggression while trying to foster a continuation of old U.S. hostility to the British Empire.

Meanwhile, as the bipartisan 9/11 Commission has made so devastatingly clear in its initial report and follow-up statements, five years after 9/11 the Bush administration has not changed U.S. institutions in ways remotely adequate to meet the threat from terrorism. It has not rethought strategy so as to meet threats from within states as opposed to from states. And when it invaded Iraq, it did so even worse prepared, and with less excuse, than the Kennedy and Johnson administrations when they went into Vietnam. Kennedy and Johnson had been told by the U.S. military that they had superbly trained anti-guerrilla forces, with a sophisticated anti-guerrilla strategy. They turned out to be wrong, but it was not unreasonable for them to believe their military advisers. The Bush administration knew very well that the United States in 2003 did not have serious anti-guerrilla forces—and did not seem to care.

In fact, with striking perversity, the Bush administration ignored all the lessons of the Cold War that would have been useful after 9/11, and chose to mimic exactly the ones that were not. In their rhetoric, they have boosted basically feeble states like Iraq, Iran, and North Korea into substitutes for the erstwhile mighty Soviet superpower enemy; and yet they have not studied how that enemy was actually defeated. Instead of making local elites stakeholders in their own revival, Ambassador L. Paul Bremer ruled from Baghdad like a viceroy and current U.S. ambassador Zalmay Khalilzad openly strolls the floors of Iraq's parliament, cementing deals between the various Iraqi factions. Too often the administration has crossed the line from facilitating into dictating, to its cost.

In particular, the Bush administration and too many Democrats have not recognized two critical Cold War lessons. The first, which was known to all the wisest Cold Warriors of the Truman and Eisenhower administrations, was that in the struggle between free market democracy and Communism, it was not enough to preach the virtues of democracy and freedom. Across the world, people had to see that siding with America brought them real advantages in terms of economic growth, jobs, services, education, and basic security.

That was clearly perceived by everyone from former socialists like Reinhold Niebuhr to President Eisenhower himself. It has been all too often ignored since 9/11.

Secondly, in much of the world, the struggle between American-backed free market democracy and Soviet-backed Communism was only partly about their inherent virtues. It was also, and critically, about which of them could appeal most successfully to local nationalism. Where America was able to appeal to a desire of nations to escape from Soviet imperial domination, America ultimately won. Where the Communists were able to portray America as imperialist and themselves as continuing an anti-colonial struggle for national independence, the Communists won—at least for a while. The most intelligent creators of the containment strategy, like Kennan, and its most intelligent intellectual backers, like Niebuhr and Morgenthau, understood this from the start. The rest of the U.S. establishment learned this lesson through the experience of Vietnam, at a cost of sixty thousand American dead and untold Vietnamese casualties.

The greatest mistake of the Bush administration, and the greatest contrast with the Truman and Eisenhower administrations, has of course been the decision to neglect the struggle with Al Qaeda and instead pursue an irrelevant vendetta against Saddam Hussein. As of early 2006, it appears to be repeating the same mistake in an even more disastrous form by threatening conflict with Iran. To use a metaphor from the Hollywood of the Truman-Eisenhower era, those presidents adopted a James Stewart strategy: They faced down the enemies in front of them, preferably without even having to draw a gun. On the other hand, the Bush administration has been the Charlie Chaplin of the international scene. They took a wild swing, hit the wrong man, and fell over their own feet.

If both the Bush administration and the Democratic Party establishment have failed to learn from Eisenhower and Truman, the left wing of the Democrats—while correct in its opposition both to many Bush policies and to the Democratic leadership—has failed to learn from Henry Wallace's failure. Too often in recent history, the

American left has seemed to criticize what America is, rather than what it is doing, while simultaneously ignoring far worse alternatives. This kind of attitude continues to bedevil it today. Because of its power among Democratic activists (though not the party establishment, which is simply promising to implement Bush policies more efficiently), this attitude contributes to the inability of the Democratic Party to develop an effective opposition to the policies and attitudes of the Bush administration and the neoconservatives.

After the Communist invasion of South Korea, Wallace publicly acknowledged that he had been wrong about the Communist threat. He pledged his support to the war effort, while continuing to condemn what he saw as excessive and dangerous Cold War policies. Like the later Wallace, the American left needs to pledge its support to the struggle against Islamist terrorism and extremism, and to the U.S. military and security forces who are carrying on that struggle. On the other hand, it should by no means abandon its principled and entirely correct condemnation of gratuitous preventive wars like the one in Iraq, and of monstrous and self-destructive measures like torture, adopted by the Bush administration and justified by too many of its supporters.

Unlike the conformist ideas now being put out by most Democratic leaders, an alternative strategic vision will have to be truly radical, and rooted in a different moral sense; but to succeed in winning support it will also have to be like the strategy of Truman and Eisenhower: both obviously realistic and visibly patriotic; devoted to American values, American pride, and the security and interests of the American people.

Among the lessons for today that can be drawn from the Truman-Eisenhower experience is that any truly successful program must be one that can rally massive support beyond America's shores. This does not mean some kind of mechanical submission to votes in the United Nations—something that would have rendered the conduct of the Cold War impossible. It does mean creating a strategic and ideological program that many non-Americans will follow without having to be dragooned into doing so.

Another measure of the success of new strategies will be their political sustainability at home. As in the 1940s and 1950s, for a strategy to be successful, beyond being right, it must have staying power, and that depends on mass domestic support. The lack of this, as revealed by more and more opinion polls in 2005 and 2006, is sapping the U.S. ability to fight on in Iraq.[42]

It is the Truman moment's successful combination of toughness, pragmatism, and moderation that we must recall today in seeking a new national consensus to support the war on terror. Such a consensus, to have any chance of political longevity, must combine elements of both traditional pragmatism and morality, as the mass of the American people understands these terms.

Today, the American foreign policy scene resembles a looking-glass version of that of Truman and Eisenhower's day, with a certain touch of Alice in Wonderland thrown in. Now as then, after a period of bitter partisan strife over foreign policy, the establishments of the two main parties have come to support what is basically the same program, even though they themselves might fiercely deny this. Now as then, those presenting real alternatives have been banished to the fringes. The difference is that today the two parties have come together behind a profoundly foolish and dangerous program, a somewhat moderated version of that put forward by the neoconservatives in the Republican Party and liberal hawks among the Democrats.

It is the exponents of utopian visions and overambitious uses of American power who have moved to center stage in both parties; and the true centrists, the moderate, pragmatic descendants of Truman and Eisenhower, who have been banished to the wings. It is because it is so necessary to end this dangerous situation that it is vital that we recall the values and positions for which Truman and Eisenhower really stood, as well as look at the ethical realist philosophy that underpinned them.

Two

THE FAILURE OF ROLLBACK
AND PREVENTIVE WAR

There is nothing more foolish than to think that war can be stopped by war. You don't prevent anything but peace.

—HARRY S. TRUMAN

Preventive War from the 1940s to Today

So completely has history vindicated containment that its opponents, the rollback-and-preventive-war school, have been not so much discredited as demolished. Just as no one seriously now claims that Stalinism was a basically benign and nonaggressive system, so no one seriously claims that it would have been right to launch a preventive nuclear war to destroy a Soviet Union that was always much weaker than it seemed and eventually crumbled of its own accord, just as Kennan and Truman had predicted.

By the time Ronald Reagan came to office, a generation after containment was put in place, the strategy had done its work as its founders had intended. In the intervening years, the Communist economic, political, and ethical model had failed for all to see—above all relative to the West. The prestige of the Communist Party and its ideology had collapsed all over the Soviet bloc. The Soviet empire was infinitely weaker than it had been under Stalin. Reagan understood how rotten the Soviet bloc had become, and acted accordingly. In doing so, he was also able to rally support from a majority of Americans of both parties. While the most important factor in the Soviet empire's collapse was its own internal decay, Reagan's policies certainly gave it an extra push.

But we should also remember that Reagan was the heir not only of containment's results, but also of its philosophy. While in his first term Reagan talked and acted very tough, this gave him the political cover in his second term to pursue an approach to the Soviet leadership that was actually rather close to Kennan's philosophy. He worked closely with Soviet leader Mikhail Gorbachev and Foreign Minister Eduard Shevardnadze to cooperate on international issues, implement radical arms control, maintain stability, and conduct a peaceful wind-down of the Cold War. For this, he was indeed attacked at the time by some of the neoconservatives.

By contrast, as historian Daniel Kelly said gently of one of the key intellectual works of the preventive war school, published by James Burnham in 1947, "the most obvious weakness of *The Struggle for the World* lay in the contrast between what it predicted and what actually happened"[1]—as, for example, with Burnham's categorical statement of 1952 that "if the communists succeed in consolidating what they have already conquered, then their complete world victory is certain. . . . We are lost if our opponent so much as holds his own."[2]

Quite apart from the likelihood that the United States—and of course the Soviet vassals in Europe whom America wanted to liberate—would have been destroyed in the process, there is the question so wisely raised by Eisenhower: Even if the United States had destroyed Russia, or China, at low cost to itself, what would it have done with the results? If the United States had done this to the Russian and Chinese populations after what they had suffered at the hands of the Nazis and Japanese, then instead of the troublesome but rational Russian and Chinese states of today, we would be facing hundreds of millions of ordinary Russians and Chinese permanently possessed of a searing hatred of the United States and an implacable desire for vengeance.

We should remember this today when thinking about how to deal with Iran. If we wait Iran out, then given the Iranian youth bulge and its apparent dislike for its elders, there seems a good chance that in a generation's time we will have a country that is once again a responsible and basically pro-Western member of the international community (though we should never expect that this will make Iranians obedient followers of American strategy). If we attack Iran, and if as is all too likely this leads to a major war and widespread destruction and civilian losses, then we will have Iran— not just the regime, but the mass of the Iranian nation—as an implacable enemy for decades to come.

And yet the preventive war school remains alive and well in America, among neoconservatives, hard-line classical realists of the Donald Rumsfeld variety, and even leading Democrats. After 9/11, it enjoyed a rebirth, and under the false name of "preemption" it has been a central element of the Bush administration's National Security Strategies of both 2002 and 2006—with no acknowledgment that this approach had been proposed and carefully analyzed once before in American history and found hopelessly wanting.

The need for "preemptive" war against a future Iraqi threat was the central justification for the attack on Iraq in 2003. Today, the same rationale is being used for calls for an attack on Iran. But let us be quite clear: This is not preemption at all. The right of states to strike preemptively in the face of imminent attack by enemy states or coalitions—as Israel struck in 1967—has always been asserted as a right by all states, America included. A claim to the right of preventive war against a state that might possibly attack you in the future is something very different and very new. It represents a revolution in international affairs, and a terrifying precedent for the behavior of other countries.

Of course, the supporters of preventive war today do not claim to be following the old preventive warriors. On the contrary, they claim to be descendants of the containment school, and in terms of personal lineage they sometimes are. But in terms of mentality, spirit, style of argument, and understanding of the world, neoconservatives like Norman Podhoretz of *Commentary* magazine are true descendants of James Burnham and General Orvil Anderson.

This is to be seen in their tendency grossly to exaggerate the power both of America's enemies abroad and of real or alleged traitors at home. Burnham and Podhoretz both portrayed the Soviet Union as so strong and American democracy as so pathetically weak and decadent that unless America went to war quickly, it might well be doomed. This recalls the old saying about the Austrian empire's disastrous decision to go to war in 1914: "Out of fear of dying, we committed suicide." Burnham may have had some minimal excuse for writing this anti-American rubbish in the late 1940s.[3] Podhoretz was still saying this kind of thing in the early 1980s, a few years before the Soviet collapse.[4]

Related to despair over America's "Athenian" democratic softness and respect for our enemies' "Spartan" authoritarian discipline has been a Teutonic obsession with power and will. Burnham wrote that in the struggle with Communism, "for us, international law can only be what it was at Nuremberg (and what it would have been at Moscow and Washington if the other side had conquered): a cover for the will of the more powerful."[5] A leading contemporary neoconservative, Charles Krauthammer, has written that

> America is no mere international citizen. It is the dominant power in the world, more dominant than any since Rome. Accordingly, America is in a position to reshape norms, alter expectations and create new realities. How? By unapologetic and implacable demonstrations of will.[6]

This obsession with showing will has had real and tragic effects on American policy in the world. In its decision to send U.S. troops to Vietnam, the Johnson administration was heavily influenced by the belief that if it failed to show will and determination there, "it might as well give up everywhere else—pull out of Berlin, Japan, South America" as Johnson himself put it.

Like many people who talk all the time about will and strength, the representatives of the preventive war tradition actually suffer from very poor nerves. They like to portray cautious pragmatists as

Chicken Littles, but in fact it is they who are forever warning that the sky is falling. They tend to turn every minor clash and threat into the crack of doom. For Burnham, a small mutiny of the Greek navy was "the beginning of World War III," and an Italian-Yugoslav squabble over the city of Trieste was the hinge on which hung the survival of the West.[7] For the neoconservatives throughout the 1990s, every petty ethnic clash in the ruins of the former Soviet Union heralded the restoration of that state as a mortal threat to the West. Weak, isolated, and despised regional states with a tiny fraction of America's power are elevated into new equivalents of the Soviet superpower, and mortal threats to American dominance.

Burnham wrote that the idea of a Cold War lasting decades was intolerable, because Western civilization could not stand the constant irritation. He never realized that constant itching is as much an inevitability of life in the international jungle—even in benign and peaceful times like the 1890s or the 1990s—as it is in a real jungle. In this sense the neoconservatives, the liberal hawks, and their ancestors are just as much utopians as the Communists used to be. They too believe in the possibility of what is in fact an impossibly stable and permanent state for the world, a kind of world democratic nirvana under American hegemony.

Most dangerous of all has been this tradition's refusal to study individual nations and local conditions. Its exponents prefer instead to treat these realities with an ideological cookie cutter, throwing away the bits that don't fit. Thus according to this approach, in the Cold War all nations had to be neatly pro-Soviet or pro-American. Today they must be pro-terrorist or pro-American.

This sometimes near-racist contempt for the values, interests, identities, and politics of different nations—especially non-Western ones—led Burnham and others into predictions and recommendations that can still cause a kind of hysterical laughter. Thus he predicted in 1947 that since the Indians were obviously incapable of governing themselves, if the British left India, that country would inevitably fall first into chaos and then into Communism. He therefore recommended that the United States take quasi-imperial power over India, as part of an American world empire that was necessary if Communism was to be resisted.[8]

From the fact that Burnham went on writing for a generation after publishing this proven and catastrophically dangerous nonsense, and that Podhoretz is still advancing apocalyptic versions of international affairs twenty-six years after writing in 1980 that the United States faced the likelihood of a choice between imminent subjugation by Moscow and war, we can say two other things about this tradition: that it is incapable of learning, and that it is without shame.

Distinguishing Between Enemies: Communism and "Islamic Totalitarianism"

Thank God, America never did try to rule India, and most of Burnham's wild ideas were likewise rejected by U.S. administrations. In one respect, however, figures like Burnham did contribute to an error that became generally shared, led to terrible consequences in the real world, and is being repeated in a new and disastrous form in our own time. This was their unconquerable belief that all Communist movements and states were identical and part of the same unified threat to the West—a belief that survived being shown, for example, that Burnham and others had been utterly wrong about Marshal Tito of Yugoslavia being simply an agent of Stalin.

Kennan wrote,

> There seems to be a curious American tendency to search, at all times, for a single external center of evil, to which all our troubles can be attributed, rather than to recognize that there might be multiple sources of resistance to our purposes and undertakings, and that these sources might be relatively independent of each other.[9]

This error stemmed, like so many other errors then and now, from a desire to divide the world into clear areas of black and white, good and evil. It has led above all to a determined refusal to study or understand the power of local nationalism, whether reflected in Communism, Islamism, or other phenomena.

This mistake led directly to America's tragic involvement in Vietnam. For that involvement was predicated on the fear of a united Soviet–Chinese–North Vietnamese move to dominate Asia. In fact, before the first Marine regiment had even set foot in Vietnam, the Chinese-Soviet alliance had already irretrievably broken up—yet, blinded by their vision of united Communism, most U.S. policymakers and politicians simply could not see this, even when the evidence was placed in front of them. As has been the case in our time, lower-level analysts in the State Department and the CIA who did see what was happening were forced to suppress or modify their views to suit the dominant consensus.[10]

Three years later, while thousands of Americans were dying in Vietnam to resist this supposedly united Communist threat, the two great Communist powers were fighting in eastern Siberia, and coming close to a nuclear clash. Later, Vietnam and China fought their own border war. These clashes meant that America had no need to fight in Vietnam at all—it could, and eventually did, contain the spread of Communism in the region by simply playing the Communist states themselves off against each other. Today, we see the equally absurd and potentially tragic situation of America pursuing a policy of implacable hostility toward Muslim states that are among Al Qaeda's fiercest enemies.

George Kennan predicted such national splits in the Communist camp from the start. So did Reinhold Niebuhr, who drew a distinction between Soviet Communism and the various Communist movements of Asia, including the Chinese and Vietnamese versions. He saw Soviet Russia as an imperial power, dominating other nations by force and terror. In Europe, therefore, the West could justly and successfully represent itself as a force for liberation. In Asia, because of the legacy of European colonialism, things were much more complicated. Communist movements there were savage and ruthless, but they could also present themselves successfully to their own peoples as forces for national liberation from

Western imperial domination. This gave them a capacity to inspire genuine mass support of a kind that did not exist in the Soviet empire outside Russia itself.

Because they recognized the importance of nationalism as a force behind many of the Communist movements, Niebuhr, Kennan, and others were also decades ahead of most of America in seeing that this also inevitably meant that Communist states would sooner or later fall out among themselves, because of old rivalries and different national interests. As Niebuhr wrote in 1948,

> A Communist China is not as immediate a strategic threat as imagined by some. The Communism of Asia is primarily an expression of nationalism of subject peoples and impoverished nations. . . . It may take a long time to prove that we are better friends of China than Russia is. But if Russia should prove as heavy-handed in dealing with China as she has with the Eastern European nations, it may not take as long as it now seems.[11]

This prediction was of course proved by history to be entirely accurate. It must be said, though, that it did not require any miraculous powers of prophecy. Even before the Korean War, the split between Tito's Yugoslavia and Stalin's empire had already shown to all with eyes to see that this was likely to be the pattern of the future. Later, their perception of the power of anti-colonial nationalism, and of the differences between different Communist movements, led Niebuhr, Kennan, and other founders of the containment school to oppose the U.S. involvement in Vietnam.

Kennan had recognized this reality in Vietnam no less than fifteen years before the start of America's full-scale military involvement. In 1950 he wrote to Secretary of State Dean Acheson that it would be disastrous for the United States to replace the French colonialists in Vietnam, and that in any case Vietnamese Communism would sooner or later become a fully national force that would not be subservient to either Russia or China.[12]

In recent years, neoconservatives and liberal hawks have come together in a disastrous repeat of the rejection of what ought to have been this self-evident reality. During the Cold War, Podhoretz continually referred to "the Communists" as if they were all the same. Today, he writes of "radical Islamism and the states breeding, sheltering, or financing its terrorist armory"—as wildly varied a bunch as one could imagine—as "the enemy," and "he."[13] This is a bit like a Brit of a former age talking about "the Hun" and "Johnny Chinaman."

Neoconservatives have been joined in this regard since 9/11 by leading intellectual representatives of the liberal hawk tendency in the Democratic Party. The confluence of the two streams is especially noticeable in a term that has been adopted and used widely by both of them, namely "Islamic totalitarianism" (also called "Islamo-fascism"). This weird and disastrous concept repeats in an even worse and less excusable form Cold War illusions about Communists all forming part of one united bloc.

Thus in his seminal liberal-hawk text *Terror and Liberalism*, the leading liberal hawk Paul Berman argues that secular radical Arab nationalism and Islamic fundamentalism are essentially the same phenomenon, since both are supposedly expressions of an anti-liberal, totalitarian international ethos and tradition stemming originally from the Europe of Fascism and Communism: "The Baathists and the Islamists were two branches of a single impulse, which was Muslim totalitarianism—the Muslim variation on the European idea," he writes.

The "global war on terror" is therefore in his view a continuation of America's past struggle against Nazism and Communism. In Berman's view,

The totalitarian wave began to swell some 25 years ago and by now has swept across a growing swath of the Muslim world. The wave is not a single thing. It consists of several movements or currents, which are entirely recognizable. These movements draw on four tenets: a belief in a paranoid conspiracy theory, in which cosmically evil Jews, Masons, Crusaders and Westerners are plotting to annihilate Islam or subjugate the Arab people; a belief in the need to wage apocalyptic war against the cosmic conspiracy; an expectation that post-apocalypse, the Islamic caliphate of ancient times will re-emerge as a utopian new society; and a belief that meanwhile, death is good, and should be loved and revered.[14]

Seeing Arab Baathism, Iranian Shiism, and pan-Islamic Sunni extremism as all part of the same movement, and the "political culture" of all the different Muslim countries as identical, in his latest book Berman still feels able—all the contrary evidence notwithstanding—to portray the invasion of Iraq approvingly as part of the struggle against Al Qaeda and the transformation not just of the Arab world but the entire Muslim world:

> The American strategists noticed that terrorism had begun to flour-ish across a wide swath of the Arab and Muslim world. And they argued that something had to be done about the political culture across the whole of that wide swath. The American strategists saw in Saddam's Iraq a main center of that political culture, yet also a place where the political culture could be redressed and transformed.[15]

Meanwhile neoconservative Michael Ledeen describes both the Ayatollah Khomeini and Osama bin Laden as "fascists," the latter because "Osama's speeches and sermons are remarkably short and melodramatic, and invariably couched in the language of war"—which would make a very large part of the Western tradition of the past two thousand years "fascist."

With the exception of a common hostility to Israel, this whole picture is a farrago of nonsense. The ideological and theological roots of radical Islamism were laid down more than a thousand years before Fascism was thought of. As to the suggestion that Sunni radicalism, Shiism, and Baathism all forms part of the same basic "movement," this is the equivalent of suggesting that in the Europe of the past, Communism, Catholic conservatism, Fascism, and Russian tsarism were all basically part of the same movement because they were all hostile to liberal democracy—a suggestion that would render most of modern European history completely incomprehensible. The "Islamic totalitarianism" argument applied to all the current strains of radicalism in the Muslim world is no less historically illiterate.

In taking this line, liberal hawks and neoconservatives have had even less excuse than American analysts did during the Cold War. For whereas the different Communist parties did at least officially subscribe to the same Marxist-Leninist dogmas and the same "scientific socialist" vision of historical progress, the chief forces in the Muslim world are fundamentally opposed to one another in their basic doctrines and in their view of history.

In the case of Sunnis like Al Qaeda and its allies on the one hand and the Shia, on the other, this has been true for 1,300 years. Radical secular Arab nationalism, as represented at its most extreme by the Baath parties in Iraq and Syria, did indeed draw on roots in European Fascism. But as anyone with the most minimal knowledge of Muslim history knows, the roots of both Sunni and Shia religious radicalism are infinitely older—dating back indeed to the first decades of Islam's existence. Even the religious culture of Al Qaeda and its allies, Salafism, derives from ancient roots in Sunni Islam; and Al Qaeda's specific theology, Wahabism, originated more than two centuries ago in eighteenth-century Arabia.

Baathism has always been deeply and often violently opposed to both Sunni and Shia fundamentalism, just as secular nationalist parties in Europe used to detest the Catholic Church. Baath Arab nationalism is deeply opposed to any attempt to restore the "Islamic caliphate of ancient times"—as dreamed of by Al Qaeda and its Sunni radical allies—because this would embrace all Muslims, and the Baathists want to create a united Arab secular state under their own fascistic rule.

In any case, the ideological founder of the Baath, Michel Aflaq, was a Christian Arab, as were some of Saddam Hussein's leading minions. As modernizing nationalists, like their former European equivalents, the Baathists also regard Sunni fundamentalists as dangerous opponents of Arab progress. As for the Shia, they were always regarded by the Baathists as not only culturally alien and retrograde, but as Iranian agents as well. In this, the Baathists were following the original Italian Fascist model that strongly influenced Aflaq.

The Fascists had their roots in bitterly anti-clerical Italian radical nationalism. When in power, like Saddam Hussein's Baath Party in the 1990s, the Italian Fascists made pragmatic deals with religion in the form of the Catholic Church; but in Italy and Germany, Fascism was never in any sense influenced by or close to the Christian religion. This does not, of course, make the Baathists or the Fascists more likable. It does make them very different from the forces of political religion.

By refusing to make this basic distinction between Arab nationalists and Islamists, Berman demonstrates the same disastrous, willful ignorance that led the Bush administration into Iraq in the belief that by overthrowing the Baathists they would also strike a mortal blow at Islamist terrorism. This applies with even greater force to the failure of Berman and others to make the critical distinction between Shiite and Sunni Islam, and between the different national agendas of Iran and various Arab states.

In terms of strategic sense, their line is equivalent to the argument that the United States and its allies should have fought Nazism and Soviet Communism not sequentially, but simultaneously. This strategy was indeed promoted by Churchill in the winter of 1939–40. If it had been followed, it would have ensured Britain's defeat and a dark age for the world. In other words, this "analysis" deliberately promotes and justifies the most dangerous aspect of the Bush administration's approach to the war on terrorism: the lumping together of radically different elements in the Muslim world into one homogeneous enemy camp. As we can see in Iraq, this has been a magnificently successful example of a self-fulfilling prophecy. It has created a perfect situation for Al Qaeda and its allies, on a scale they could never have achieved without massive U.S. help.

Americans for Democratic Action

Since 9/11, the liberal hawk advocates of this disastrous school of thought have tried to appropriate the memory and teachings of Reinhold Niebuhr, in a way that radically misinterprets his real views on U.S. strategy and indeed by far the greater part of his philosophy.

This ideological dress-up game takes the form of attempts to revive for their contemporary purposes the image of Americans for Democratic Action (ADA). This was a movement that Niebuhr helped to create in 1947, and that played a critical part in the late 1940s in rallying American liberals to support the Truman administration, oppose Soviet Communism, and support its containment by firm American action. Among the founders of the ADA were Eleanor Roosevelt, John Kenneth Galbraith, Arthur Schlesinger, Jr., and Hans Morgenthau.[16]

The ADA's founders had previously led in the struggle to persuade Americans to abandon isolation and join in the fight against Nazi and Japanese aggression. They recognized far earlier than most the essentially new and especially dangerous character of the mid-twentieth-century totalitarianisms. They came to extend their previous struggle against German Nazism to Soviet Communism— though like Kennan they were always clear that these were in many ways different threats, and that the methods used against them would therefore also have to be different. As Schlesinger wrote, the ADA helped to "fundamentally reshape" American liberalism, dropping its former tendencies toward pacifism and isolationism and committing it to international struggle against totalitarianism and aggression.[17]

Reviving the spirit of the ADA was the main theme of an essay by Peter Beinart, then editor of *The New Republic,* in December 2004, entitled "A Fighting Faith: An Argument for a New Liberalism." On this he also based a book that appeared in 2006.[18] Beinart and other liberal hawks have called on American liberals and

Democratic Party supporters to fight a "worldwide crusade for democracy" against "totalitarian Islam," just as the ADA fought against totalitarian Communism.[19]

Beinart supported the Iraq War, like Paul Berman, Leon Wieseltier, Thomas Friedman, Christopher Hitchens, and other leading Democratic intellectuals. These figures are both influential in their own right and closely tied to the Democratic Leadership Council, and to dominant figures within the Democratic Party's foreign policy leadership, including Senators Hillary Rodham Clinton and Joe Biden, former secretary of state Madeleine Albright, and Ambassador Richard Holbrooke.[20]

In his 2006 book, Beinart puts some new distance between himself and the more hard-line liberal hawks, and brings his arguments a bit closer to those of the real ADA, rather than the propaganda reconstruction of it that has been put together in recent years. For example, he continues to use the term "Islamist totalitarianism," but now makes clear that by this he means only the Salafi tradition from which Al Qaeda has sprung. He no longer—in this book at least—attempts to extend this term to cover the Shia or radical Arab nationalists.

In certain respects we welcome and respect such positions, and see them as one part of a desirable process of bridging the outdated, irrelevant, and damaging party political divide over foreign policy. For the same reason, we also welcome the new views of Francis Fukuyama—another ideological semirepentant, in his case from the neoconservative camp.

In an ideal world, these positions would gradually converge in a new consensus that would provide real answers for America's pressing challenges and real help in the struggle against Al Qaeda and its allies. We especially approve of Beinart's commitment to equitable development as right in itself and also an essential part of the war on terror—something on which Truman, Eisenhower, and the ADA all agreed. We also agree with him on the need for the American left to develop a new sense of critical patriotism, and above all a new commitment to the armed forces.[21]

In the real world, however, Beinart and even the more moderate and sensible liberal hawks still have a long way to go. It is very good that Beinart now admits that he was wrong to support the war in Iraq. This mistake he ascribes mainly to what *The American Prospect* has rightly called "the incompetence dodge"—the argument that the liberal hawks could not possibly have predicted the extent of the Bush administration's incompetence.[22]

However, Beinart's new approach is also linked to a new and belated recognition of part of the core of Niebuhr's message: the inherent limits on all human power and wisdom; and the particular need for America, although generally in the right, to recognize that it is also capable of great wrong, and to observe limits on its behavior accordingly. The problem is that when it comes to the recognition of "limits," such liberal hawks are still all too representative of much of the establishment in general. As a result of the Iraqi debacle, they have become more cautious, but not necessarily much wiser. Beinart writes of limits, but then, like the Bush administration's National Security Strategy of 2006 (NSS 2006), repeatedly comes back to his belief in America's mission to democratize the world.

In his presentation, however, this mission is now supposed to be achieved not through the United States acting unilaterally, but through an "alliance of democracies." In the circumstances this can only mean European democracies, with the possible addition of Turkey, Israel, and India. Here Beinart reveals the central problem of the liberal hawk school when it comes to the war on terror, which is an indifference verging on autism toward the views of the Muslim world in general, and the Arab world in particular.[23]

From the point of view of most Arabs, this "alliance of democracies" would simply mean replacing "American imperialism" with "Western imperialism." The addition of India and Israel just suggests to Muslims a global anti-Islamic alliance. And even the presence of Turkey is not much help, given bitter Arab memories of Turkey's role as the former imperial power in the region. In other words, arguing for this kind of American strategy completely ignores the role of nationalism in the countries concerned. This blindness to the national feelings of other peoples is a disastrous flaw in present U.S. approaches—not only to the Muslim world, but to much of the outside world in general.

As the analysis of the "Islamic totalitarianism" line reveals, too much of the liberal hawk and neoconservative view of the Middle East—and, alas, of American perceptions in general—is overwhelmingly self-referential. Although ostensibly about backing Muslim liberals and defeating extremists, it is not really linked at all to real debates in the Muslim world.

In this too the proponents of a Cold War–style ideological struggle against "Islamic totalitarianism," along the lines of the ADA's struggle against Soviet-backed Communism, have been guilty of a basic misunderstanding of the differences between the Cold War and the war on terror. This misunderstanding applies not only to the liberal hawks, but to much of the American establishment in general. It has been responsible for the creation, with bipartisan support, of the U.S. Arabic-language propaganda stations Al Hurra TV (the "Free One") and Radio Sawa. These were founded on the explicit model of Cold War propaganda stations like Radio Liberty and Radio Free Europe—a model that is in fact completely irrelevant to the Arab world.[24]

For the early years of the Cold War were not only a struggle against Soviet expansionism; they were also an ideological civil war within Western Europe, and to a lesser extent within America. Karl Marx was a German. Although Communism triumphed spontaneously only in Russia and Yugoslavia, it came close to doing so at various times in Hungary, Germany, Spain, France, Italy, and Greece. For long periods, Communist parties had genuine appeal to the masses, and still more to the intelligentsia—especially, of course, when they were fighting against Fascism. Even more dangerously, the Communists often showed immense skill at forming "popular fronts" with social democratic and even liberal parties. These fronts had a democratic appearance, but were used by the Communists as a cover for their plans to seize all power for themselves and create totalitarian "dictatorships of the proletariat."

The ADA was founded precisely to counter moves toward such a popular front in the United States, and to reach out to democratic forces in Western Europe to help them resist Communist blandishments. Instead of lumping all socialist movements together as enemies, the ADA appealed in particular to the non-Communist European left—and this became the official strategy of the Truman administration, and the covert one of the CIA.[25] So in the mid-twentieth century, the struggle for the soul of the progressive Western intelligentsia was indeed critical to resisting Communism and Soviet expansionism.

The struggle with Sunni Islamist radicalism is quite different. Beyond a very few individual converts, Islam in general, and its extreme Salafi and Wahabi forms in particular, have no appeal whatsoever to the Western masses or intelligentsias. Islamist extremism does have a dangerous presence in the West, and especially in Western Europe—but this is through support among the Muslim immigrant minorities. Disaffection among these minorities is a serious problem, but unlike in the case of the Communists, it does not pose a threat of revolution and the seizure of the state.

The ideological struggle against Al Qaeda and Islamist radicalism is therefore one that can only be conducted by Muslims themselves. Unlike the leaders of the ADA, the liberal hawk intellectuals are completely irrelevant to this struggle—or, rather, worse: Insofar as they display a mixture of arrogance and ignorance toward the Muslim world, and support U.S. and Israeli policies that even liberal Muslims generally find detestable, such American intellectuals are actively dangerous. Thus U.S. official aid to Iranian liberal groups, far from helping them, is destroying their credibility in the eyes of most Iranians.

In other words, we must not allow the preaching of democracy, as advocated by neoconservatives and liberal hawks alike, and as embodied in the National Security Strategy of 2006, to go on getting in the way of tough but informed and enlightened diplomacy. This spirit of diplomacy animates the philosophy of ethical realism, which was developed by Niebuhr, Morgenthau, and Kennan, and which we describe in the next chapter.

Three

ETHICAL REALISM

History is blind, but man is not.

ROBERT PENN WARREN, *All the King's Men*

By heeding the core teachings of ethical realism—prudence, patriotism, responsibility, study, humility, and "a decent respect" of the views and interests of other nations—the United States can fashion a new strategic vision, which we call the Great Capitalist Peace. This vision can help in the struggle against Al Qaeda and its allies and provide the basis for a consensual and stable international order.

Ethical realism is tough enough to provide a basis for the harsh actions that the United States may well need to take in the future to defend itself, its values, and its allies. But unlike some strands of "classical" realism, it is not cynical, indifferent to the long-term interests of humanity, or attracted to ruthlessness for its own sake. It is rooted in the commonsensical, everyday morality and generosity of spirit that Americans practice themselves and expect of their neighbors.

We need to bring morality in American statecraft down from the absolutist heights to which it has been carried, and return it to the everyday world where Americans and others do their best to lead ethical lives while facing all the hard choices and ambiguous problems that are the common stuff of our daily existence. This includes a shrewd awareness that the people who talk the loudest about their own morality are not always those who practice it the best; and that people are judged not only by what they say they are doing or will do in the future, but by what they have said and then done in the past.

By these standards, it is deeply foolish to expect Arabs or Iranians to trust the United States, and still less Britain, when we say that we are now motivated by a genuine desire to bring democracy to their region, and not by a desire for domination, control of oil, or other self-interested motives. Given our past record, and all the times in the past when our rhetoric has proved hypocritical, why on earth should they trust us—even if on this occasion we may in fact be speaking sincerely?

This is all the more so when—as advocated by Charles Krauthammer and others and expressed in NSS 2006—the United States openly adjusts its public conscience according to its geopolitical advantage, talking loudly about democratic morality in cases that suit it, while remaining silent on others. In NSS 2006, the Bush administration loudly condemns lack of democracy in semi-democratic Iran, while praising democratic progress in totalitarian Saudi Arabia, for example. Can this by any normal standard be called a moral approach? Would we listen to a neighbor, or a religious preacher, who so flagrantly adjusted his principles to suit his advantage? Of course, we can still work to promote democracy in the region over time, but we must be very careful to accompany this effort with policies that visibly serve the interests of the peoples concerned, and are tailored to their wishes. Otherwise, many people in the world will go on rejecting U.S. initiatives even when they are genuinely well intentioned.

The modern ethical realists all believed in America and America's mission, but they were all deeply troubled by the self-deceiving, morally arrogant, and even messianic tendencies in the United States, and where they might lead. The theologian Reinhold Niebuhr declared that "there is only one empirically provable element in Christian theology, namely that 'All have sinned and fallen short of the glory of God.' " He reminded us of the lessons of the Old Testament:

The prophets never weary of warning both the powerful nations and Israel, the righteous nation, of the judgment which waits on human pretension. The great nation, Babylon, is warned that its confidence in the security of its power will be refuted by history. . . . Israel [in the Bible] is undoubtedly a "good" nation as compared to the nations surrounding it. But the pretensions of virtue are as offensive to God as the pretensions of power. One has the uneasy feeling that America as both a powerful nation and a "virtuous" one is involved in ironic perils which compound the experiences of Babylon and Israel.[1]

Morgenthau wrote,

Political realism refuses to identify the moral aspirations of a partic- ular nation with the moral laws that govern the universe. . . . The light-hearted equation between a particular nationalism and the counsels of Providence is morally indefensible, for it is the very sin of pride against which the Greek tragedians and the Biblical prophets warned rulers and ruled. The equation is also politically pernicious, for it is liable to engender the distortion in judgment which, in the blindness of crusading frenzy, destroys nations and civilizations.[2]

Morgenthau was a secular intellectual but one steeped in the Old Testament—and perhaps equally important, in memories of how the moral self-righteousness of German nationalist culture had helped lead that country to repeated catastrophe in the first half of the twentieth century.

A Call to Civil Courage

As Niebuhr's warning suggests, the origins of ethical realism are ultimately religious, though today this philosophy operates dis- tinctly from these roots. The philosophical bases were laid down by St. Augustine almost 1,600 years ago; and at the heart of this philosophy—whether represented by a Christian theologian like Niebuhr, a Christian agnostic like Kennan, or a secular Jew like

Morgenthau—remains the central question set out by Augustine: How can we live and work in the City of the World while being as true as possible to the City of God?[3]

As Augustine taught, to live and act for the good in the City of the World is an ethical duty, but to do so effectively requires a realistic view of human nature and human society. Any other approach points in the end toward utopian fanaticism or academic seclusion, to the revolutionary firing squad or the monk's cloister. Thus Niebuhr condemned the American left for insisting that if the United States could not act with perfect purity, it should not act at all. The result, he said, would be a catastrophic abdication of international responsibility.[4]

Yet if human states will always act in the end according to their own self-interest, individual statesmen have to remain under some influence of conscience, or the world will quickly go to hell. They have to serve the national interests of their states, but they must also try both to make their states act in ways that will serve the good as far as possible and to observe certain strict limits as to what they are prepared to do on behalf of their states. For as Niebuhr observed, man is a lion—a ferocious and carnivorous animal—but he is also "a curious kind of lion who dreams of the day when the lion and the lamb will lie down together."[5] In other words, acknowledging reality does not mean approving that reality, or abandoning the duty to try to change that reality for the better.

As developed over the years by generations of Western thinkers, this Augustinian tradition raises questions for us all that transcend the specifically Christian message: How can we work for a better world in an inevitably imperfect one? How can we maintain this kind of effort while knowing that we can only ever succeed to a very small degree in reaching our goals, as these are defined by our values? How can we reconcile working for practical success in this world—with everything that this implies of compromise—with keeping some fidelity to higher ideals? Recognizing that all practical action involves some element of sin, how do we prevent that recognition from becoming an excuse for cynicism and amorality? When claiming to be true to our higher ideals, how can we try to make sure that we are not in fact just using them as a cover for personal or national aggrandizement? And finally, how can we reconcile loyalty to our family, clan, or country—loyalties that are in themselves ethical, and that can be real and living forces for good—with loyalty to our ethical ideals, or to God?

Niebuhr tackled some of these central dilemmas as follows, while being quite clear that his approach represented a way of looking at the problem, rather than a universal formula for resolving it:

> It is possible for both individuals and groups [including nations] to relate concern for the other with interest and concern for the self. There are endless varieties of creativity in community; for neither the individual nor the community can realize itself except in relation to, and in encounter with, other individuals and groups. . . . A valid moral outlook for both individuals and for groups, therefore, sets no limits to the creative possibility of concern for others, but makes no claims that such creativity ever annuls the power of self-concern or removes the peril of pretension if the force of residual egotism is not acknowledged.[6]

Ethical realism therefore poses these essential questions while understanding that they can never be fully or permanently answered, and that there can never be any definitive reconciliation between these two sets of demands; that in every separate case a new ethical decision will have to be made, depending on the special circumstances, and that in every case the possibility exists that this decision will be wrong either practically or ethically. There can never be finality or closure, except in death.

The conduct of international affairs in an ethical realist spirit therefore requires leaders with a combination of open minds, profound moral convictions, and strong nerves. Moral convictions alone, not combined with open minds, lead to fanatical rigidity. Open minds without a moral foundation can lead to cynical and shortsighted opportunism. And even a combination of an open mind and a moral foundation will not be enough if the leader concerned does not have the moral courage to make clear and tough decisions. To be sure, this is a very rare combination, but it is a combination exemplified by the characters of both Truman and Eisenhower, and which we must hope that America will produce again in the future.

Ethical realism recognizes that in the great majority of humanity, impulses to good and evil are mixed up together. As George Kennan wrote in answer to Quaker pacifist criticism of the containment strategy:

> It is idle to suppose that just because we human beings have our redeeming qualities and our moments of transcendent greatness, we are "nice people." We are not. There are many times and situations when we require restraint. . . . It would be a luxury, admittedly, to be able to dispense with violence. But this is a luxury which man, in his present state, cannot permit himself. He is not that good. His responsibility is not that small.[7]

Ethical realism therefore embodies a strong sense of the fundamentally tragic nature of the human condition. Its vision is not purely tragic, however, because it also believes in the ability of men and nations to transcend in spirit their circumstances and to strive toward the good, though never fully to achieve it. In this, ethical realism differs from much of "traditional," or "classical," realism, whose exponents also have a tragic sense but too often ignore both moral factors and the possibility of domestic progress, and believe that in the end, states, and the relative power of states, are the only really important imperatives on the international scene.

The tragic sense inherent in ethical realism brings with it a call to the greatest and most essential of all republican and democratic virtues, which is moral courage: the courage to confront this existential uncertainty, and yet to act firmly for the right, "as God gives it to us to see the right," in Abraham Lincoln's words. It requires us to make this kind of decision again and again, with all the moral agonizing and hard practical work that comes with such decisions. As Morgenthau wrote,

> We have no choice between power and the common good. To act successfully, that is according to the rules of the political art, is political wisdom. To know with despair that the political act is inevitably evil, and to act nonetheless is moral courage. To chose among several expedient actions the least evil one is moral judgment.[8]

Morgenthau was cautiously respectful of Machiavelli's harsh realism, but he also wrote that "it is a dangerous thing to be a Machiavelli. It is a disastrous thing to be a Machiavelli without virtu," a term embracing the values of duty and honor as well as physical and moral courage.[9] Both Niebuhr and Morgenthau described the greatest American president, Abraham Lincoln, as exemplifying this kind of moral courage among his many other virtues.[10]

For this reason, ethical realists have always had a certain disdain—being ethical, they would never admit to outright contempt—for those thinkers who evade this hard thinking and these hard choices by taking refuge in all-embracing, all-answering ideologies and their attendant myths: whether the old Communists who believed that Marxism-Leninism had the answer to every major problem and that these would be resolved in a future socialism; or the Democratists who believe the same thing about an idealized and ideologized version of "democracy"; or the nationalists who evade all these issues by simply identifying democracy, freedom, truth, justice, and goodness with their own nation. Thanks to the collapse of their would-be socialist utopias, the old-style Marxists are now pretty much out of it; but the Democratists, the nationalists, and above all a mixture of the two are alive and flourishing in the United States today.

Against the soothing appeal of these utopian illusions, ethical realism's call to moral and civil courage is of especial importance in contemporary America. Many of the hard practical decisions that need to be taken in order to place U.S. global strategy and leadership on a safer, firmer, and more successful footing are desperately unpopular with powerful groups in our society. Advocating these changes risks severe damage to career, income, reelection, and reappointment. In view of these personal risks, the failure of the U.S. establishment to make these hard choices is human and understandable. Nonetheless, after 9/11 and its revelation of the frightful danger to American and world civilization from terrorism, and with courageous U.S. and allied troops facing death in action, the American people have the right to expect more from those who are sworn to serve their interests. This is especially true after the truly frightening experience of the national debate—or rather lack of one—before the launching of the Iraq War. During those crucial months, all too many elected representatives, state officials, and public commentators who in private expressed deep misgivings about the push for war failed to say any of this in public, essentially out of fear. And in the spring of 2006 a similar experience seems to be repeating itself with regard to the looming prospect of a U.S. attack on Iran.

The Tenets of Ethical Realism

The elements of ethical realism differ in the works of its greatest exponents, though less so than sometimes appeared at the time. Of the three, Niebuhr was the most explicit both in asserting ideas of international morality and of deriving them from ultimately transcendent sources. He always stated clearly that national interests had to be qualified by universal ethics, and that "abstract and pretentious idealism" could not be cured by "national egoism."[11] By contrast, Kennan and Morgenthau, in their polemics with American idealists, sometimes suggested that there are in fact no values beyond national interests.

However, even a cursory reading of Kennan and Morgenthau makes clear that their thought was in fact permeated by ethical considerations, even if these were sometimes "smuggled in through the back alley," as international relations scholar Robert C. Good has written.[12] This central moral element in their thought became more overt as a result of the Vietnam War, which they joined Niebuhr in opposing, and during which they were horrified by the immorality of many American actions.

Kennan himself repeatedly acknowledged Niebuhr's formative influence on his own thought. Morgenthau's and Kennan's very conceptions of foreign policy and diplomacy were suffused with moral purpose, directed toward reasonable compromise, the creation of a just and stable international order, and respect and tolerance for others. Although they derived their principles from different philosophical and religious roots, Niebuhr, Kennan, and Morgenthau shared a belief in the values of modesty, prudence, moderation, and tolerance, leading in practical terms to a preference for negotiation over violence whenever possible, and a belief in peace as the necessary basis for human progress. All agreed with Edmund Burke that "circumstances (which for some gentlemen pass for nothing) give in reality to every political principle its distinguishing color, and discriminating effect. The circumstances are what render every civil and political scheme beneficial or noxious to mankind."[13]

As a result, their public positions on policy questions were almost always very close. They all strongly supported (and in the case of Kennan, crafted) the containment of the Soviet Union, but became alarmed at what they saw as the excessive militarization of this strategy, as well as the fanatical messianism that came to infuse many American Cold War attitudes. They all categorically rejected preventive war. With varying speeds, they all came to support coexistence with the Soviet Union. While supporting sometimes ruthless measures in the struggle with Soviet Communism, they all deplored ruthless measures without real justification in necessity, like the U.S.-backed coup in Guatemala in 1954. And in consequence of the same stance, they all opposed U.S. involvement in Vietnam.

Had they lived, there can be no doubt that Niebuhr and Morgenthau would have joined with Kennan in denouncing the key policies of the Bush administration and the neoconservatives. All would have assented to Morgenthau's statement that

> The equation of political moralizing with morality and of political realism with immorality is itself untenable. The choice is not between moral principles and the national interest, devoid of moral dignity, but between one set of principles divorced from political reality and another set of principles derived from political reality.[14]

Like Morgenthau—like Acheson, for that matter—Niebuhr and Kennan were practical moralists, concerned with adopting moral positions that would actually lead to positive results, not make themselves or America feel good.

Believing that the behavior of all states is chiefly—though not exclusively—determined by their interests, the representatives of the ethical realist tradition do not believe that states can be simply divided into "good" and "evil" ones, along the lines of President Bush's infamous "axis of evil" speech. Even states with truly evil systems, like Stalin's U.S.S.R., have certain legitimate interests that will need to be recognized if peace is to be preserved in the short term. In the long term, even highly ideological regimes with revolutionary agendas, like the Soviet Union and Communist China, are also likely to be based on nations that have permanent, non-ideological national interests that will need to be accommodated if international peace is to be preserved.

Both Niebuhr and Kennan in their different ways were close to Morgenthau's notion of a "cosmopolitan ethic" binding the representatives of different states in a common responsibility for peace and order—an idea that linked him, and them in turn, to the intellectual and practical architects of the various attempts at a "concert of Europe" in the century before 1914—efforts that ultimately failed in 1914, but until then had helped to give Europe the most peaceful and prosperous century it had ever experienced. This "cosmopolitan ethic" involves in turn a sense of humility in each of the participants, and a willingness not only to accommodate the legitimate interests of others where possible, but to acknowledge their right to build different kinds of states. It is true that the European concerts were designed by European aristocrats (including an ancestor of one of the authors) with broadly similar backgrounds and cultures; but globalized capitalism is creating twenty-first-century elites who also have a good deal in common, in terms of their culture but, much more important, in terms of of their stake in the stability and success of the global capitalist order.

The great ethical realists were well aware—long before the U.S. involvement in Vietnam—that "good" states can also be capable of great evil. Morgenthau grew up in a Germany wrecked in part by the vengeful policies pursued by Britain and France after the First World War. Niebuhr came from an anti-imperialist tradition, and his awareness of the ability of democracies to commit great crimes was sharpened by the atrocities committed by French forces during their colonial wars in Vietnam and Algeria from 1947 to 1963 (and by the British in Kenya, though this was less well known at the time).

It should be remembered too that their spiritual ancestor, Edmund Burke, though one of history's greatest scourges of revolutionary extremism and Democratist utopianism, was also a committed and courageous critic of imperialist conquest, exploitation, and injustice, both in his defense of the American colonies against George III's administrations, and in his defense of the old Indian order against the ferocious depredations of the British East India Company. It is a great pity that Burke is not around today, to tear apart not only the self-serving pretensions of Democratism, but also the attempts of crony capitalist firms like Halliburton and others to use Democratism as a cover in Iraq for reenacting the behavior of the East India Company.

All of the ethical realists lived in the shadow not only of the Holocaust and of Communist mass murder but of Hiroshima, Nagasaki, and Dresden. They had to wrestle with this memory and with the possibility that a U.S. administration, out of a sincere desire to defend democracy, would begin a nuclear war in which tens or hundreds of millions would die and civilization itself would be destroyed. They shared the view of Truman and Eisenhower that while democracy must be defended, and a nuclear deterrent against Soviet aggression was essential to that end, avoiding a nuclear war—even one that the United States would "win"—was also an absolutely prime moral and practical imperative of U.S. strategy.

That meant that defense of Western democracy and containment of Soviet expansionism had to be combined with compromises intended to reduce genuine Soviet fears and accommodate legitimate Soviet security interests. In his original Long Telegram, Kennan, as noted earlier, called for a very tough policy of resisting and ultimately destroying Communist revolution and Soviet expansionism, but he also stated clearly that the Russian people were not permanent enemies of the United States, and that over time the United States needed to engage with them respectfully. In the years before his death, Kennan became a strong opponent of the expansion of NATO, and of moves to destroy Russian influence in the other states of the former Soviet Union. He regarded this as both contrary to America's real national interests and bound to provoke a dangerous Russian response.

In the ethical realist view, therefore, international relations are and always will be neither a simple struggle of undifferentiated "good guys" against "bad guys," nor some kind of predestined process leading to the permanent liberal capitalist nirvana of Fukuyama's imagining, but what Cardinal Richelieu called "a continual negotiation." The first task of ethically responsible statesmen therefore is not to seek rapid ideological transformations, but to manage international relations in such a way that this continual negotiation contributes to the maintenance of "a community of reason," in another phrase of Richelieu's.

That said, all the great ethical realist thinkers were passionately committed to Western democracy and its defense against a variety of totalitarian and aggressive enemies. They were also U.S. patriots who believed firmly in "the great coin of the liberties that we so dearly cherish," and in the United States as the supreme exemplar of democratic civilization in the world, and the most important force in defending democracy.[15] Morgenthau wrote that

> The American purpose carries within itself a meaning that transcends the natural boundaries of America and addresses itself to all the nations of the world. By pursuing its own purpose and in the measure that it achieves it, America gives meaning to the inspirations of other nations, and furthers the awakening and achievement of their purpose.[16]

But as men profoundly shaped by the experiences of the 1920s and 1930s, all the great ethical realists were bitterly aware that democracies planted in barren soil, those associated with national defeat and economic misery and unable to provide basic goods to their populations, will inevitably fail; and that in failing, they may give birth to systems far more monstrous than a traditional authoritarian system would have been: "Lilies that fester smell much worse than weeds."

Working in the shadow of the Great Depression, they were also well aware that the foundations even of Western free market capitalism, and therefore of Western democracy, are a great deal less secure than the boosters of the 1920s had assumed, or than Thomas Friedman and his flock assume today. With a profound awareness both of Western history and of the world outside the democratic West, they also realized that across much of that world, masses of ordinary people would put either material security or national independence and dignity above the achievement of Western-style democracy under U.S. hegemony.

All of the great ethical realists therefore shared the belief that while existing democracies in the world must be defended, the chief force for spreading democracy to new areas was not U.S. power, but

America's inestimably valuable example as a successful, prosperous, just, pluralist democracy. All were deeply concerned by the ways in which America failed in this in their own day, as with McCarthyism, racial segregation, and the Vietnam War with its attendant hysterias. It is not difficult to imagine their reaction to what the Bush administration has done to America's example.

For ethical realists, the world is just much more complicated than the black-and-white, good-and-evil vision of President Bush and his supporters. Niebuhr, Morgenthau, and their allies also had a keen awareness of the limits on America's ability to change the world. While the ethical realists recognized the need for military force in a world of armed states, and as an essential defense against aggression, and while they greatly respected America's servicemen, they abominated glorying in military power for its own sake. Niebuhr believed that while Christians could carry a gun when necessary, "they should carry it with a heavy heart."[17]

The Key Virtues of Ethical Realism

A foreign and security policy shaped by ethical realism would therefore differ radically from the recent approaches of both the Bush administration and the Democratic establishment. It would be far more prudent, while remaining determined to fight whenever the United States or its key allies are actually attacked, or are in real and imminent danger. It would replace the hectoring and bullying of other nations with a genuine respect for their views and interests—while remaining committed to defend the vital interests of the United States. Perhaps most important, it would be deeply patriotic, while shedding the extremely dangerous illusion that a mixture of power and goodness allows America to act at will in the world. The central principles of ethical realism must be reinvigorated to create a viable alternative to the ruinous policies followed by the Bush administration and agreed to by all too many Democrats.

Prudence

In the Christian tradition, prudence is given first place among the cardinal virtues, and for that reason used to be one of the most popular names for the daughters of New England. Morgenthau quoted with approval Edmund Burke's statement that "prudence is not only the first in rank of the virtues political and moral, but she is the director, the regulator, the standard of them all." He referred to prudence as "the god of this lower world."[18]

Morgenthau added, "There can be no political morality without prudence . . . without consideration of the political consequences of seemingly moral action."[19] Ethical realism therefore leads to prudence in shaping goals and deciding on actions. In the words of Owen Harries (founding editor of the distinguished foreign policy journal *The National Interest*), it leads to the conclusion that "the morality that is appropriate to, and can be sustained in, the soiled, selfish and dangerous world of power politics is a modest one, whose goal is not perfection—not utopian bliss—but decency."[20] Prudence stems in part from another key ethical realist virtue, that of humility, or modesty—including humility concerning our ability to understand the outside world, foresee the future, and plan accordingly.

For obvious reasons, prudence applies especially to the launching of military operations. And it is now blindingly obvious that the launching of the Iraq War violated the most basic rules of prudence, including the elementary one, set out in official U.S. military doctrine, that you must always have a Plan B in case things do not turn out according to Plan A. As we now know, there was quite simply no real plan to replace the Baath state that the United States was going to destroy.

This irredeemable, inexcusable failure encompassed a range of others. There was no plan to control public unrest and looting; there was no plan for counterinsurgency; there was no plan to secure

Iraq's borders; there was no plan to deal with ethno-religious violence; there was no plan to engage the real representatives of the
Shia majority. There was not even a plan to protect the nuclear
materials at the Tuwaitha power station from falling into the hands
of terrorists—something that this whole war was supposed to
have been about! And the clique who planned the war failed to
make these plans despite formal warnings by experts on just these
subjects in the intelligence community and the State Department—
warnings that were deliberately ignored.[21]

This was not just some intellectual or administrative miscalcula-
tion, but a profound ethical lapse. American and British lives were
staked; and American and British lives were unnecessarily lost,
along with much greater numbers of Iraqis. In recklessly failing to
prepare for entirely predictable developments, of which they had
been officially warned by General Eric Shinseki and others, the
planners of this war failed in their moral duty as public servants
and as the fellow citizens of the men and women whose lives they
threw away. In failing to exercise their duty of oversight and
informed comment, all too many members of the U.S. Congress,
the media, and think tanks failed in their moral duty as public representatives and intellectuals.

The central element of imprudence in neoconservative and liberal hawk thinking, however, extends far beyond Iraq, indeed to the
entire globe. In 1999, Robert Kagan and William Kristol produced a
showcase collection of essays on U.S. strategy by themselves and
fellow leading neoconservatives of which former British diplomat
Jonathan Clarke correctly remarked,

> Far from looking for ways to take the toxicity out of international
> problems, the authors purposefully seek out trouble spots (the
> Taiwan Strait, North Korea, Iraq) and then reach for the gas
> can. "Quiet diplomacy" or "keeping one's powder dry" are anath-
> ema. "Steely resolve" is the watchword, with the emphasis on steel.
> Indeed, it is hardly an exaggeration to say that if the book's com-
> bined recommendations were implemented all at once, the US
> would risk unilaterally fighting at least a five-front war, while

simultaneously urging Israel to abandon the peace process in favor
of a new no-holds-barred confrontation with the Palestinians.[22]

The Bush administration, supported by many Democrats, has in
effect followed a modified version of this strategy. It has simultaneously sought to destroy Al Qaeda and its allies; to stabilize
Afghanistan and prevent a return of the Taliban; to invade and
transform Iraq; to block Iran's nuclear program while also changing the regime there; to continue to give almost unqualified support
to Israel in its struggle with the Palestinians; to spread a combination of democracy and support for U.S. policies in the Middle East;
to roll back Russian influence in the former Soviet Union; and to
modify China's economic policies while supporting Taiwan and
making preparations to contain China. Achieving just one of these
goals would have been a major challenge. Trying to achieve all of
them simultaneously is a recipe for failure everywhere.

This approach to the world has also involved almost complete
indifference to what future generations may well see as by far the
greatest real contemporary threat not just to capitalist civilization,
but to modern civilization in general: namely the threat of climate
change. A detailed examination of this issue is both a subject for a
different book and beyond the consensus achieved by the authors
of this one. However, it should be clear that elementary prudence
dictates taking this threat very seriously indeed, given the warnings of the scientific community about the terrible dangers that it
could pose.

It is precisely because America is good that the present failure
to confront severe global challenges, and the imprudent fritter-
ing away of its military, economic, and diplomatic power, are so
immoral. Being a good steward of what one has been given, in
order to leave the world as good for one's children as one found it,
or better, is the bedrock of the ethical realist creed, separating what
is morally convenient from what is essential. Prudence leads to the
safeguarding of resources for when they are absolutely needed. It is
the single most important ethical trait a state's leaders can possess

in order to prepare for short-term crises and to resist long-term historical decline.

Humility

National humility, and the tolerance and patience that stem from it, were emphasized as essential virtues by all the ethical realists. Kennan wrote of "moral modesty" as central to the creation of a decent and well-ordered world, and to "that tremendous task of learning, and of helping others to learn, how man can live in fruitful harmony."[23]

Niebuhr composed the Serenity Prayer later adopted by Alcoholics Anonymous: "God grant us the serenity to accept the things we cannot change, courage to change the things we can, and the wisdom to know the difference." This is a basic tenet of ethical realism—to have any real chance of changing the world one must understand both the limits on one's ability to do so, and the limits to one's own morality. Given the drunken ambitions of today's neoconservatives and liberal hawks, they could do worse than to memorize this prayer.

While America is a force for good in the world, it isn't perfect. It has over time made grave errors and had significant moral lapses. The more American policymakers advance the idea—and believe it themselves—that America can do no wrong, the greater the risk of further errors. Diplomatically, the only result of such an infuriating stance will be its success in uniting much of the world against America, as current public diplomacy polling numbers attest.

In most disputes, we may well assume that the United States will mostly be in the right, but unless one believes that the United States is always and inevitably right, there is nothing in basic ethics or logic to suggest that its side in disagreements will always be the moral one, or that compromise is impossible with the rest of the world.

One variant of a famous American toast goes, "My country, right or wrong—but still my country." This is a rational statement of patriotism. By contrast, the suggestion that "my country is always right" is just imbecilic. Yet it is in effect the line put out explicitly by neoconservatives like Krauthammer. He holds the position that "moral suasion is a farce" and that American freedom of action and pursuit of national interest must remain absolute, utterly unconstrained by the wishes or interests of other nations, and subject only to America's own will and its own definition of morality.[24] As a moral position, this only makes logical sense if it is founded on the explicit presumption that America can do no wrong; that it is so absolutely good as to be above human judgment and restraint, not only by foreign nations but by Americans who do not fully share this faith in their country.

The extreme and explicit version of this sentiment is held by a limited number of hard-line nationalists. However, in a milder and more implicit form it is very widely held indeed. A small example of this attitude is to be found in a March 2006 report of a task force chaired by former Democratic senator and presidential hopeful John Edwards, and former Republican congressman Jack Kemp. The group was set up by the Council on Foreign Relations, a bipartisan establishment institute, in March 2006 to comment on the decline in U.S.-Russian relations.

In seventy-six pages of hectoring criticism of Russia, there is not one suggestion that any U.S. action toward Russia over the past fifteen years has been in any way wrong or harmful. Of course, Russia has been largely to blame for the decline of the relationship; but exclusively to blame, for everything? And this group included not just former U.S. officials, but supposedly independent scholars.[25] This kind of nationalism carries with it grave dangers for both morality and practical policy. For if America—or any other nation— is indeed absolutely good, opposing nations must necessarily be evil; and if virtually the whole world opposes the United States on certain issues, why then the whole world must be evil and only America good. This is the horribly unreal, unethical, and irrational position to which an unexamined belief in absolute American virtue can too easily lead.

And indeed, neoconservative professions of a desire to bring democracy to other nations are all too often strangely combined with a snarling hatred and contempt for the peoples whom they say they trust to exercise that same democracy. Krauthammer tells us that: "The world apparently likes the U.S. when it is on its knees. . . . The search for logic in anti-Americanism is fruitless. It is in the air the world breathes. Its roots are envy and self-loathing— by peoples who, yearning for modernity but having failed at it, find their one satisfaction in despising modernity's great exemplar. On September 11th, they gave it a rest for one day. Big deal."[26]

In ethical realism, by contrast, a sense of both individual and national modesty and limits is linked to a capacity for toleration. Niebuhr wrote of the "biblical paradox" that Christians have access to the truth, but also have to recognize that as mortal beings in a fallen world they can never possess it fully:

> Our toleration of truths opposed to those which we confess is an expression of the spirit of forgiveness in the realm of culture. Like all forgiveness, it is only possible if we are not too sure of our own virtue. Loyalty to the truth requires confidence in the possibility of its attainment; toleration of others requires broken confidence in the finality of our own truth.[27]

By the same token, humility leads to an ability to see one's own nation as others see it—a capacity that in everyday human morality and interaction is generally seen as positive and attractive, while its opposite is seen as not merely unattractive but also somewhat ridiculous.

The self-awareness of ethical realism embodies a sense of national history, with all its lights and shadows. As Senator J. William Fulbright wrote during the Vietnam War, "Only a nation at peace with itself, with its transgressions as well as its achievements, is capable of a generous understanding of others."[28] This emphatically does not mean that the United States or other Western countries should go around the world apologizing constantly for real or alleged past crimes. Niebuhr was quite clear about this when it came to the crimes of the European empires, which in many cases were so mixed up with their positive achievements, and with the equal or greater savagery of their enemies, as to be past conclusive judgment.

But apology for the past and awareness of the past are two very different things. Without some sense of the latter, it becomes impossible to understand the motivations of other nations—friends as well as enemies—and how they are likely to react to American policies and actions. It becomes impossible, in other words, to devise realistic policies toward them, in the sense of policies that stand some chance of success without conquest or outright coercion.

Instead, sincere efforts are needed to live up to the clarion call in the Declaration of Independence to show "a decent respect to the opinions of mankind." Taking the opinions of other nations into account and accommodating their interests when possible, beyond making ethical sense, will also help buy the United States the international goodwill in the world that it desperately needs.

Study

Ethical realism has an acute awareness of the limits of the individual's capacity ever to fully understand the world in which we live—an awareness that also leads to prudence in action. Niebuhr explicitly opposed the belief on the part of both Communists and liberals in his own time that human affairs could be grasped with the help of a simple, universal set of ideas, leading to a one-size-fits-all approach to the challenges of foreign policy.

Morgenthau, moreover, made the duty to study other countries a central ethical command. This is especially true of countries in which the United States wishes or needs to become closely involved, and where its actions are likely to have a profound impact. In Morgenthau's words,

While the act cannot be just, save by remote coincidence, the act, to be successful, cannot be without an element of justice. That is particularly true of the political act. The requisite element of justice pertains to the intellectual sphere. The successful political act presupposes a respectful understanding of its object, its nature, its interests, its propensities and potentialities. The political actor . . . must put himself into the other man's shoes, look at the world and judge it as he does, anticipate in thought the way that he will feel and act under certain circumstances.[29]

As Daniel Ellsberg, the former Pentagon official who became a leading antiwar critic, and others have remarked, not one of the senior civilian and military planners of America's engagement in Vietnam could have passed a midterm freshman examination in modern Vietnamese history. The same type of criticism could be made of the planners of the Iraq War—and this lack of knowledge is absolutely inexcusable in ethical terms. And how can anyone possibly justify the fact that of the staff recruited by Paul Bremer to help him in his administration of Iraq, only one had any background at all in the Middle East?[30]

Of course, U.S. policymakers and analysts cannot be expected to have studied in detail every country on the face of the earth. But if someone recommends that the United States intervene in another society to change its government, then not to have studied that country before recommending such an intervention is a dereliction of duty. And if this intervention risks the loss of many lives, including those of American soldiers, then this failure on the part of policymakers is morally shameful. And even more shameful is not making the effort to learn from one's mistakes.[31]

Morgenthau had an acute sense of how even the very best and most objective information and analysis available to governments and publics will have been filtered through repeated sets of prejudices, on the part of the original informants, the reporter, and the analysts. He wrote that reason is like a lamp that cannot move anywhere by its own power, but is carried around on the back of our prejudices. That does not excuse us from the duty of doing our very best to acquire accurate information and to analyze it objectively. But it means that we always have to be very careful about accepting information at face value—once again an exercise of prudence. And here we are speaking of conscious accuracy and analysis. There is also always the possibility of unconscious self-deception, deliberate manipulation and misinformation by governments, intelligence services, and the media, of the kind that occurred before both the Vietnam and the Iraq wars.

Things are still worse, of course, when even the initial information available is very limited: by a lack of human intelligence on the ground; by a lack of informed reporting from Muslim countries from diplomats forced by the terrorist threat to shelter behind ever-higher embassy walls; and by an acute lack of U.S. journalists stationed on the ground around the world.[32]

Pakistan, for example, has been widely described in the United States as "the most dangerous place on earth," because of its mixture of nuclear weapons, state weakness, and popular support for Islamist radicalism. Yet with the exception of the news agencies, not one single American media body has a regular correspondent stationed in the country. Leading academic experts on that country seem all to be over the age of sixty. The result is that if—God forbid!—the United States ever has to intervene in Pakistan, it will do so, just as in Iraq, in utter ignorance of what it is getting itself into.

Study and reporting in themselves are not enough, however. Morgenthau also echoed the advice of Atticus Finch to his daughter in *To Kill a Mockingbird:* "You never really understand a person until you consider things from his point of view. . . . Till you climb into his skin and walk around in it." In other words, you need not just intelligence and hard work but also a sympathetic and creative imagination.

From this point of view the situation in the West is quite appalling, and is being made much worse by the self-serving illusions of Democratism. Statements by Bush, Britain's prime minister Tony Blair, and their supporters to the effect that "these values of freedom are right and true for every person, in every society" (National Security Strategy 2002) are self-evident rubbish. Two hundred years ago, when British and American society and culture were very different from what they are today, so were British and American attitudes toward freedom, and indeed to every other social value. We can be sure that two hundred years from now, they will be very different from ours today. There is no reason therefore in either logic or charity to think that it is natural, inevitable, or necessary that very different cultures and societies in the world today must naturally share the same beliefs and values as the United States and Great Britain.

As a result of these attitudes, among the enormous numbers of analysts in Washington still employed in the study of Russia, the number who are actually capable of placing themselves in the skins of most Russians can be counted on the fingers of one hand. They themselves, of course, sincerely believe otherwise. But that is because the Russians whom they know well, and feel they understand, have been selected and self-selected to confirm American attitudes and prejudices. Those Russians who disagree just do not get Western grants and jobs, and are not interviewed as "serious" and "objective" sources of analysis by Western journalists.

Mostly, this copulation of illusions is just designed to secure individual financial and career benefits for the West's local informants. But it also continually lays the U.S. establishment open to manipulation by the likes of Iraqi opportunist and neoconservative darling Ahmed Chalabi for their own political ends. Indeed, several leading Washington think tanks are virtual nurseries for flocks of Baby Chalabis, all mewling into the doting ears of their foster parents about how the freedom-loving people of Ubangi-Gangi or Khakistan love America, support American policies, want America to intervene in their countries to "restore democracy"—and above all, want their beloved Ahmed Junior to get back his old job as minister for corruption. You think we exaggerate? Look at Benazir Bhutto's record in office, and then ask how large parts of the U.S.

establishment can possibly believe that her return to power would be good for Pakistan.

Responsibility

Ethical realism embodies what the German social scientist Max Weber called the ethic of responsibility, as opposed to the ethic of convictions; or between a morality of results and a morality of intentions. Ethical realism's acceptance of a morality for statesmen that is more flexible than the morality for individuals stems above all from a recognition that the immense responsibility of statesmen to the communities they serve is a moral imperative that needs to be balanced against other moral imperatives.

Under an ethic of responsibility, having good intentions is not remotely adequate. One must weigh the likely consequences and, perhaps most important, judge what actions are truly necessary to achieve essential goals. An ethic of conviction, while superficially moral, has a tendency to be indifferent to the consequences of actions in the real world.[33] And even when the will to take action is there, neither in statecraft nor in common sense can good intentions be a valid excuse if—as in the decision to go to war in Iraq—they are accompanied by gross recklessness, carelessness, and indifference to the range of possible consequences.

Among the questions to be studied is whether your country, its forces, and its resources are really strong enough to achieve the aim in view; whether your government and military are competent enough to achieve it; and whether your own people really have the will to remain committed to a given country or conflict for the time that will be necessary to stabilize it—which in turn reflects the question of whether their vital interests are truly engaged there.

Ethical realism does not seek to evade responsibility for necessarily ruthless actions or to whitewash their cruelty. It does, however, insist that these actions, and the strategies of which they form a part, should be truly necessary. For example, Niebuhr argued that the massive Allied bombardment of cities in Germany and Japan was morally defensible, but the American bombardment of civilians in Vietnam was not.

Indeed, a certain capacity for ruthlessness in making such moral choices lies at the heart of ethical realism, though ruthless action is only acceptable if it is truly necessary in defense of the country or of higher human goals against threats to civilization itself. As Burke said, it all depends on the circumstances. The Allied bombardment of Germany and Japan was part of a necessary war to preserve humanity from the twin scourges of Nazism and Japanese militarism. On the other hand, Niebuhr, like Morgenthau, Kennan, and many of the other founding members of the ADA, opposed the war in Vietnam not so much for its cruelty but because they rightly saw the war as irrelevant or even detrimental to the basic struggle against Soviet Communism. Its cruelty had no moral justification in necessity.

Similarly, the authors of this book supported the war in Afghanistan and came to oppose the war in Iraq. But that was not because we thought that the first war would be somehow clean and humane. On the contrary, it was obvious from the first to every honest person who knew anything of Afghanistan that war there was going to be an ugly business. Unless we were to flood the place with our own troops—which would have been logistically impossible and politically disastrous—we were going to have to rely on ground troops provided by an exceptionally nasty bunch of drug-dealing Afghan warlords and ethnic militias, whose forces moreover had the most bitter wrongs to avenge on the Taliban. Even when the initial killing was over, the subsequent guerrilla war has also inevitably proved a vicious one, with considerable civilian losses from U.S. bombing, and human rights abuses both by U.S. forces and those of the Afghan quasi-state that the United States and it allies created. We say "inevitably" because every guerrilla war of modern times has involved such abuses, regardless of whether the state forces involved came from "dictatorships" or "democracies."

Of course, this does not absolve states from seeking to limit abuses, and differences of degree remain important. The fact that U.S. forces in Iraq and Afghanistan have so far committed many fewer atrocities than they did in Vietnam, or the Russians have in Chechnya, reflects credit on them and their commanders. Nonetheless, anyone who calls for his country's soldiers to engage in a guerrilla war needs to have the moral courage to assume responsibility for the abuses that will inevitably follow, and to be able to marshal really convincing arguments for the necessity of that decision. We believe that given the nature of war and of Afghanistan, many of the civilian deaths in that conflict have been unavoidable, and justified. By contrast an ethic of convictions (or "ultimate ends")—especially when linked to the belief that one's nation is the representative of all that is good—has a dangerous tendency to excuse its proponents from responsibility for the consequences of their actions, because "their heart is in the right place."

The point about the moral difference between abuses in the Afghan War and those in the Iraq War therefore is not that the first were better, but that the first war was justified, and the second was not. In our view, the Afghan War met all the traditional moral and legal standards of a just war, as derived from the classical and Christian traditions and preached by ethical realism. It was not a war of choice, but a response to an attack; it was proportionate to that attack—as it would not have been if, for example, U.S. forces had carpet-bombed Afghan cities; and it was supported by the international community.

None of these standards was met by the Iraq War, and in consequence its abuses must be judged unnecessary and gratuitous. The difference, if you like, was between a police officer who accidentally kills a pedestrian while speeding to catch a criminal who has just murdered someone, and a similar death caused when the policeman only thinks that the suspect—who admittedly has a very bad previous record—might be planning to commit a crime in the future. Public opinion and common sense would judge the first death to be regrettable, but also excusable; and the action of the policeman in the second case to be unjustifiable, and above all, irresponsible.

Patriotism

The last of the great ethical realist virtues is patriotism—and it should be remembered that for the generations of Niebuhr, Morgenthau, and Kennan, patriotism really meant something, not only for the masses but for the elites. The children of those elites volunteered and died in disproportionate numbers in both the First and Second World Wars. A return to this kind of patriotism on the part of the political and intellectual elites is necessary if the United States is going to be able to go on making the military sacrifices that will be required of it from time to time as part of its global role.

All of the ethical realist figures we have studied were profoundly patriotic, and attached to the interests, the values, and the honor of their country. The values of American patriotism are indeed inestimable, and have been demonstrated by their ability over the years to attract the passionate allegiance of generation after generation of new immigrants to America, from the most diverse possible national and cultural origins.

Here, though, an important distinction must be drawn between patriotism and nationalism. Irving Kristol, one of the fathers of the neoconservative movement, has expressed this difference very well, in declaring that the neoconservatives must consider themselves to be nationalists, and not patriots:

> Patriotism springs from love of the nation's past; nationalism arises out of hope for the nation's future, distinctive greatness. . . . The goals of American foreign policy must go well beyond a narrow, too literal definition of "national security." It is the national interest of a world power, as this is defined by a sense of national destiny.[34]

This is a statement that explicitly links neoconservatism with the tradition of the French Revolution, in the fires of which modern mass nationalism was born. It brings out the way in which nationalism has always been attached to visions either of struggling for an ideal future or a return to an ideal past. Kristol looks to a future vision of America. Other extreme nationalists have looked back to an idealized past, and declared, with the mid-twentieth-century French radical rightist Charles Maurras, that "to love France today, it is necessary to hate what she has become."[35] Both tendencies have shared an indifference or even hostility to their country, and countrymen, as these actually exist. For the sake of such imaginary visions, nationalists have been prepared to make almost limitless sacrifices of the treasure and blood of their real, existing countries, and their real, living compatriots.[36]

Patriotism by contrast is attached to a country and its people as they actually exist, warts and all. In the Anglo-American tradition, it is linked to Burke's idea of a ladder of loyalty beginning with the "little platoon" of your family, and then ascending upward to your country and its institutions, at every stage based on a loyalty to real people and concrete things. Truman and Eisenhower certainly loved their country, but more important they also liked their country, and this acted as a check on any temptations that they may have had to gamble with its existence for the sake of fantasies of absolute security, world dominance, or universal democracy.

From the point of view of ethical realism, it is important that this kind of patriotism is not only a spur to duty, service, honesty, and self-sacrifice but can also be a force for an international "community of reason"—something to which nationalism, and especially messianic neoconservative-style nationalism, is directly contrary. An enlightened patriot expects the citizens, and especially the public servants, of other countries to be patriots too. He or she does not expect that they will ignore their loyalty to their country and instead identify with American interests just because the United States claims to represent the ideals of world Democratism, or with Soviet interests (in the past) because the Soviet Union claimed to represent world Communism.

American officials must both pursue national interests and seek to set those interests within a framework that will be beneficial for humanity in general. It can also rule out certain kinds of international behavior, such as aggressive war, deliberate targeting of civilians, torture, subversion of established local elites, and so on—though if it wants patriots of other nations to respect these rules, it had better follow them itself. What it cannot do is expect that these patriots will sacrifice their own vital interests without compensation, any more than the United States itself would do.

Viewed through this prism, many international issues take on a very different appearance than that usually presented by the U.S. media and commentariat. Thus the United States can demand that Russia rule out certain kinds of methods in trying to maintain its influence over countries in the former Soviet Union. But it cannot demand that Russian officials abandon that influence over a region of vital interest to Russia, any more than the United States can reasonably be asked to abandon its influence over Central America. A public figure who advocated this would be regarded by most Americans as little better than a traitor—remember when just this accusation was hurled at Jimmy Carter over his willingness to give (even very theoretical) sovereignty over the Panama Canal Zone to Panama?

Similarly, America can legitimately demand that Iran break its links to terrorist groups, cease making inflammatory statements about Israel, and accept strict international supervision of its nuclear facilities. What it cannot do is expect that Iranian patriots, in a country surrounded by nuclear-armed states, should abandon the possibility of a nuclear deterrent without receiving concrete security guarantees and other compensation for their country in return. A U.S. official who recommended such action by America in similar circumstances could not just be legitimately accused of treason but charged with it in court.

An enlightened patriotism therefore fuses with the other virtues of ethical realism to produce the flexibility, calm, and perspective necessary if the United States is successfully and peacefully to carry on its present role as the world's leading state. The messianic Democratist nationalism of the neoconservatives and liberal hawks tends to infuse international issues in which the United States is involved—even the most morally ambiguous, or the least important to U.S. interests—with a terrifying self-righteousness, and thereby to make their reasonable solution vastly more difficult.

By contrast, the virtues of ethical realism would help U.S. policymakers to create a hierarchy of interests, and then to decide which ones are truly vital and which ones can be adapted so as to accommodate the vital interests of other states. The principal virtues of ethical realism form part of the essential foundations of the Great Capitalist Peace, a concept that we will explore in the next chapter.

Ethical Realism and American Strategy

Ethical realism is therefore of universal and eternal value for the conduct of international affairs, and especially useful as a guiding philosophy for the United States and its war on terror. As we pointed out in the Introduction, the American people quite rightly expect their representatives to conduct a realistic and tough defense of their interests, but most also expect those representatives to observe certain moral limits and to seek a higher good not just for America but for humanity.

Following 9/11, a messianic commitment to spread Democratism has become the keystone of America's political strategy in the war on terror. But the Bush administration, and some of its backers in the Congress and media, have also adopted ultrarealist methods—including torture, kidnapping, aggressive war, indifference to civilian casualties, and contempt for even democratically expressed international opinion. This kind of radical inconsistency has badly damaged America's reputation for honesty and good faith—which is just as much a part of America's international credibility as are tanks or aircraft carriers.

In a way that Niebuhr in particular recognized and warned against, messianic idealism combined with nationalism has also fed a ruthlessness in some quarters, because as with so many other ideologies—

even good ones—it has led to a feeling that America is so good that anything it does is somehow justified. In Kennan's words of 1951, while idealists are devoted in principle to the elimination of war, in fact their fanaticism often "makes violence more enduring, more terrible, and more destructive to political stability. . . . A war fought in the name of high moral principle finds no early end short of some form of total domination."[37]

Soon after the Kennedy administration's abortive attempt to overthrow Fidel Castro in 1961, by backing a Cuban opposition invasion of Cuba at the Bay of Pigs, Undersecretary of State Chester Bowles commented in his diary,

> The question that concerns me most about this new administration is whether it lacks a genuine sense of conviction about what is right and what is wrong. . . . Anyone in public life who has strong convictions about the rights and wrongs of public morality, both domestic and international, has a very great advantage in times of strain, since his instincts on what to do are clear and immediate. . . . The Cuban fiasco demonstrates how far astray a man as brilliant and well-intentioned as Kennedy can go who lacks a basic moral reference point.[38]

This, of course, was at a time when Kennedy and his followers were thrilling Americans and many others by their ideological language of a commitment to spreading freedom and democracy. But Bowles was talking about something different, and ultimately more important: the individual moral conscience, based on firm and sound principles, that seeks to judge every action in moral terms. These terms may well include that of how far the action involved serves an ultimately moral purpose, such as victory in the struggle against Soviet Communism. But this moral purpose must in each case be supported by concrete evidence, and be subject to reasonable debate. It cannot simply be inferred from general propositions such as that America is good and America's enemies bad, and therefore anything done by America in the struggle against them must be justifiable.

In the case of the Bay of Pigs invasion, such a debate had to include not only whether the operation stood a reasonable chance of success, but whether Castro's regime was really either a close ally of the Soviet Union (before the U.S.-backed intervention), whether it was really a serious threat to the United States, and whether even in the event of the invasion's success, the likely damage to America's reputation, to America's interests elsewhere, to international law, and to the Cuban people justified any likely gain. Similar questions needed to be asked before the invasion of Iraq, and need to be asked before an attack on Iran.

In debates of this kind, an ethical realist approach to U.S. policy would help to bring the ethical, the practical, and the idealistic elements of the U.S. tradition back into some kind of cooperative harmony. In doing so, ethical realism can also make both realism and idealism much more practically useful for the struggle against terrorism and extremism.

When it comes to formulating an overall approach to this struggle, on the basis of ethical realism we condemn U.S. Democratist idealism for the wholly unrealistic time frame it sets for the development of stable democracy; for its indifference to the social, economic, and cultural changes necessary to underpin democracy; and for its bizarre belief that democracy elsewhere in the world necessarily equals support for American foreign policy.

However, on the same basis, we condemn classical realism in the style of Henry Kissinger and former national security adviser Zbigniew Brzezinski. This philosophy has been widely and justly criticized for its obsession with states, its tendency to see states and nations as unchanging, and therefore its indifference to internal developments within them. And of course this kind of realism has been attacked by ethicists of every stripe—including ethical realists—not only for its lack of a sense of ethics in the conduct of policy, but also for its lack of any sense of the long-term goals of that policy, beyond a short-term defense of the national interest and a temporary status quo that favors that interest.

In the struggle with terrorism, this kind of realism falls short because by far the greatest terrorist threat to the West is not from states, which even if vicious can be deterred, as the Soviet Union was deterred, but from internal extremist developments within states, as a result of their social, economic, and political decay. Combating that decay, and developing these societies, is therefore an essential part of the struggle against terrorism.

The Bush administration claims to be pursuing this approach, but as we shall argue in the following chapters, if U.S. strategy in this regard is to have any effect, it requires a far deeper and longer commitment of both money and of political and bureaucratic attention than anything the administration has attempted or its neoconservative backers have advocated—or, indeed, than is being put forward by the leadership of the Democratic Party.

Four

THE GREAT CAPITALIST PEACE

For what shall it profit a man, if he shall gain the whole
world, and lose his own soul?

GOSPEL OF ST. MARK, 8:36

One of the chief duties of any empire should be to keep its eye
on posterity. That is to say, to create an image of its values and
achievements so attractive and inspiring that they will continue to
shape humanity long after the empire itself has disappeared.

The Roman Empire managed this so magnificently that even
today, almost 1,600 years after the fall of Rome, legal systems
based on Roman law continue to govern much of humanity—
including peoples the Romans never encountered and could scarcely
have imagined. The achievements of the China's Han Empire and
its Confucian ideology were such that after that empire's death it
remained directly relevant for almost two millennia, with each
new Chinese dynasty declaring itself the heir of the Han and the
restorer of the Han system.

We do not know how the British Empire will be remembered
a millennium from now. However, it is clear that so far, and in
the case of India, Malaysia, and some other former dominions, the
impact of British parliamentary government, British law, and the
British civil service continues to shape those countries decades
after Britain ceased to rule them. At a speech at Oxford University
in 2005, the Indian prime minister, Manmohan Singh—himself an
Oxford graduate—declared,

Our notions of the rule of law, of a Constitutional government, of a free press, of a professional civil service, of modern universities and research laboratories have all been fashioned in the crucible where an age old civilization met the dominant Empire of the day. These are all elements that we still value and cherish. Our judiciary, our legal system, our bureaucracy and our police are all great institutions, derived from the British-Indian administration, and they have served the country well.[1]

By the time he spoke, of course, Britain by contrast retained not one scrap of actual physical power or hard geopolitical influence over India.

But this kind of influence was never just about power. The Mongol empire, for example, was larger and more powerful than any before the British, but after its demise nobody remained influenced by its legal, administrative, or cultural legacy—or at least, not in a positive way. Outside Turkey and Russia, few of the former subjects of the Ottoman or Soviet empires recall their systems with much affection.

In other words, the influence of the American system on the world is something that should be seen as greater and more important than raw power. This system comes in two parts. The first is America's own example as a state and society, embodying liberal democracy, the rule of law, a successful market economy that distributes its benefits widely in its population, and, more broadly, "the American way of life." The second part of the system has been America's role in crafting an international market system that on the whole—and it is on the whole that such great historical factors must in the end be judged—has served humanity well.

Direct American power has often been critical to this achievement, as in the defeat of the Nazis and Japanese, and the containment of the Soviet Union. But it has not always been central. The transformation of Central Europe in the 1990s was made possible initially by a mixture of the European Union's accession process and American security guarantees.

By far the greatest improvement in human well-being in recent decades has been through "Communist" China's adoption of its own form of the free market. This was a process that owed everything to a mixture of America's free market example and America's shaping of a global market economy—but nothing to any direct exercise of American power. The same is true of India's decision in the 1980s and 1990s to abandon its previous quasi-socialist system and adopt successful market reforms.

And this distinction between American power and the American system holds true to a degree even for Americans themselves. As Michael Lind argues in his brilliant book *The American Way of Strategy* the most important thing for America has been not the pursuit of international power for its own sake, but power insofar as it is necessary "to defend the American way of life by means which do not endanger the American way of life."[2]

If this is so, it follows that the American way of life is threatened not only directly, by enemies such as Nazi Germany and the Soviet Union, who seek to destroy it; but also indirectly, by the danger that, in mobilizing to resist these and other enemies, America will become a "garrison state" like those of Europe in the past, and will lose its own soul. As George Washington warned, "Overgrown military establishments . . . under any form of government, are inauspicious to liberty, and . . . are to be regarded as particularly hostile to republican liberty."[3] Concern with this danger from within has deep roots in the American tradition, and in the British tradition that gave it birth. As we have seen, both Presidents Truman and Eisenhower feared this. Eisenhower famously declared, in his farewell address of January 17, 1961,

This conjunction of an immense military establishment and a large arms industry is new in the American experience. . . . We recognize the imperative need for this development. Yet we must not fail to comprehend its grave implications. Our toil, resources, and livelihood are all involved; so is the very structure of our society. . . . In the councils of government, we must guard against the acquisition of unwarranted influence, whether sought or unsought, by the military-industrial complex. . . . We must never let the weight of this combination endanger our liberties or democratic processes. We should take nothing for granted. Only an alert and knowledgeable citizenry can compel the proper meshing of the huge industrial and military machinery of defense with our peaceful methods and goals, so that security and liberty may prosper together.[4]

The threat of America becoming a garrison state has been enormously increased by 9/11 and the resulting increase in domestic surveillance. This need is in part real, but it should also be clear that some of the measures that have been proposed or implemented put significant civil liberties in peril. These include the Secret Service becoming a virtual praetorian guard; the administration's wildly expansive view of the power of the executive branch, so far largely unchecked by Congress; the arrest and prolonged detention of hundreds of Muslim residents, often on the flimsiest of charges; the warrantless wiretaps of American citizens; and torture at Iraq's Abu Ghraib prison and elsewhere.

By this token, America could retain and even expand its present global power while still losing most of its beloved values, habits, and even institutions, which are the foundations of the American system and of America's legacy to the future. Equally, Americans could experience a calibrated reduction of their global power while still retaining their cherished way of life.

America can only carry out such a reduction, however, if the global market system as a whole and its complement, basically civilized relations between major powers, remain more or less intact. Otherwise, the dangers to America itself would be too great. The preservation of this system from its various enemies is therefore the most important task of U.S. statecraft. American power is a means to that end, not a goal in itself.

The Example of the British Empire

In contemplating a future world in which U.S. power is used more effectively but in more limited ways—indeed, more effectively because of these limits—Americans can also draw upon the example of British strategy in the century before 1914, when its global power was at its zenith. This experience has been used by writers such as Niall Ferguson and Max Boot as an example for the exercise of American global power today and in the future.[5] Such recommendations too often ignore the fact that British power even at its height was in certain key respects limited; and that at the start of the twentieth century Britain conducted a deliberate strategic withdrawal from several regions in order to concentrate on what London regarded—rightly—as its most dangerous enemies.

Britain's directly ruled empire was also not the heart of its economic supremacy. More important was Britain's indirect influence over large parts of the globe, and above all its domination of the world economy through its lead in industry, technology, trade, and finance.

This Great Capitalist Peace of the nineteenth century can be updated and advanced as an alternative American strategy for the new era. This alternative depends on America as global leader, and therefore ultimately upon its military and economic strength, and upon American will. It does not, however, require America to be an empire, or even the global hegemon. It does not depend on dominating the whole world militarily, and being able to launch victorious wars all over the globe against a range of different states. On the contrary, at the heart of this idea is the creation of a network of major states, all of which have a vital economic and security stake in defending the existing order. America, will, of course, retain enough military power to defend its own vital interests, but it will take care not to threaten those of other regional powers, unless primary American interests are genuinely threatened. Like the United States today, the British Empire played the leading role in opening and protecting the international commons (safe trade, open sea-lanes, and the suppression of piracy/terrorism). This role benefits the global power both directly and by providing benefits for other countries, which are then more likely to support the ordering power's leading global position. Britain "also derived a great deal of its staying power from the perception of cultural superiority,"[6] as Zbigniew Brzezinski writes—a perception that existed even in a grudging fashion among many rebels against the British Empire.

Today, American universities, especially at the graduate level, are the envy of the globe. As a result, many of the most talented foreign students flock to the United States, where they imbibe American culture firsthand. The United States is far and away the number-one film and television exporter to the rest of the world. From jazz to Bogart to Homer Simpson T-shirts, from the sublime to the absurd, the rest of world literally buys into America in a way that it does no other country.[7]

The economic pull of British power also matched its cultural assets. In 1860 Great Britain accounted for 53.2 percent of world manufacturing output, a bit more than America's share in 1945. The unchallenged global reach of London—militarily, politically, and commercially—gave Great Britain a strong vested interest in keeping trade relations open and free.

There is another subtle yet equally important advantage that emanated from Great Britain's economic superiority and consequent advocacy of free trade—once again, the benefits that flowed to other countries from such a policy. Trade is never a zero-sum game: Many countries and the world in general benefit from the overall prosperity that an increase in free trade brings. Great Britain's advocacy of a more open world gained it political acquiescence from other states for its dominant global role, as benefits flowed well beyond Great Britain itself. Its economic policies won over countries that might otherwise have chosen to challenge British supremacy.

Because of Britain's stake as the global economic, financial, technological, and cultural leader, the British Empire generally functioned as a conservative, status quo power in its relations with the other major states. It was interested in preserving the existing world order, and not in gratuitously picking fights with other great powers except in the cases where this was regarded as necessary to the protection of truly vital British interests.

The military aspect of British global supremacy was founded primarily on the Royal Navy, which according to British strategic doctrine was supposed to be (and until the 1890s usually was) at least as strong as those of the next two great powers combined. Like that of the United States today, Britain's naval superiority gave it a colossal advantage when it came to "lift"—the ability to transport large numbers of troops across much of the world quickly and safely.

However, if Britain's nineteenth-century strengths resemble those of America today, so do some of its key weaknesses. Because the British recognized this, and tailored their strategy accordingly, they managed to remain the dominant power until the crippling losses of the First World War. For, whatever its naval strength, on land Britain was the weakest of all the major nineteenth-century powers except for the United States. For this reason, Britain could never intervene unilaterally on the continent of Europe. It always needed to put together a coalition of powerful allies.

Equally important, after 1815 Britain never intervened in North America. For although the U.S. armed forces were weak, in the Revolutionary War and the War of 1812 Britain had learned two severe lessons about the ability of American society to generate large numbers of determined volunteers, and about the way that America's size and geographical isolation rendered British naval superiority of very limited use.

By the second half of the nineteenth century, America's colossal latent strength already made it difficult for London to think of launching a land war in North America, for the almost inevitable result would have been the loss of British Canada. So the British were content that the United States should remain a neutral power, tied into Britain's world system through British investments in the United States and American interest in British guarantees of international trade and financial stability.

In the entire century from 1815 to 1914 the British only launched one significant military operation on the European continent, in the Crimean War—and even that was on the farthest periphery of the continent, and was only possible because the French and the Turks provided the bulk of the ground forces.

The reasons for Britain's particular weaknesses during the nineteenth century were basically the same as those for America of today. Above all, both the British and the American populations have been deeply hostile to the conscription necessary to create armies large enough to fight prolonged wars with major powers and establish armies of occupation, and to the taxes necessary to pay for huge armies and endless wars. Britain therefore conquered and ruled its empire through a mixture of professional troops and local native auxiliaries and mercenaries, and in consequence deliberately restricted its ambitions to weak Asian and African polities that could be conquered with relative ease.

The difference is that in the case of the United States today, the demilitarization of society has gone so far that it is difficult to raise even volunteer troops for long and bloody overseas wars. Volunteer armies are also much more expensive than conscript ones. In the case of both Britain and the United States, the resulting fiscal strain has been made worse by the fact that as global, not regional, powers, they have also had to maintain immensely expensive navies (and in the U.S. case, an air force) and the high-tech industries to build them. Like the United States now, Britain then was by far the richest power on earth, but that did not mean that its resources were infinite.

Britain's nineteenth-century strategy, then, was an economical one, intelligently tailored to the British Empire's real strengths and weaknesses. London did not seek to acquire global dominance of the kind now being dreamed of by U.S. neoconservatives and liberal hawks. It always recognized that Britain had to coexist in the world with a number of other great powers, each with its own sphere of legitimate interest, which it would be reckless folly to meddle with.

During the 1890s, Britain's economic predominance disappeared in the face of the dramatic growth of the American and German (and to a lesser extent, Russian and Japanese) economies. In part for inexorable geographic and economic reasons, and in part for domestic political ones, the British government failed to check this relative economic decline—just as it may not be possible for any U.S. administration to do much about the relative economic rise of China.

What they could and did do in the British case was to take a cool, levelheaded look at the strategic implications of these developments, and adopt radically new strategies to deal with them. Recognizing that to try to remain predominant everywhere would mean risking defeat everywhere, British policymakers identified the threats to Britain's truly vital interests and prioritized accordingly. They ceded predominance in Latin America to the Americans, and Britain signed an alliance with Japan that essentially recognized that country as the predominant power in the Far East. A few years later, in 1907, as the menace of Wilhelmine Germany grew, Britain signed a treaty with its old rival Russia that guaranteed British rights in southern Persia but surrendered predominant influence over the country to St. Petersburg.[8] As historian Paul Kennedy has written,

Much of the public rhetoric of British imperialism does not suggest that concessions and withdrawals were the order of the day. But the careful assessment of British strategic priorities went on, year after year, examining each problem in the context of the country's global commitments, and fixing upon a policy of compromise or firmness.[9]

None of this was easy for a British official class that had been used to dominating all these regions for generations, and expected to be ferociously criticized for these withdrawals by sections of British opinion. This strategy of limited strategic retreat took not just intelligence but great moral courage. Without this willingness to conduct painful compromises and tactical retreats in the twenty years before 1914, Britain would undoubtedly have been defeated in the First World War.

U.S. Power—Global but Limited

The very idea of reducing America's presence in any area of the world is anathema to most of the foreign policy establishment. As Eisenhower warned, their own narrow interests as a ruling elite are completely against this; they have also convinced themselves that it isn't necessary. Amazingly, even after the savage lesson of Iraq, one can still frequently hear in Washington, from representatives of both parties, the line that "U.S. power in the world is practically unlimited."

Of course, in certain narrow military fields, such as naval and air supremacy, and the ability to deploy precision-guided munitions against identifiable objects, this is true, just as it was true that for most of the nineteenth century, the Royal Navy could destroy at will most of the other navies in the world. The figures are well known. The United States spends as much on its military as the rest of the world put together. It has the only large aircraft carriers in the world, and the only forces widely equipped with precision-guided missiles and bombs.

True—but also frequently irrelevant. The British could knock over any army outside Europe and North America—but they could not generate the forces to occupy and rule a vast civilization like China. The United States today can knock over any army and regime with relative ease—but it cannot occupy and change societies such as Iran, Pakistan, or even little Iraq. The Royal Navy could not help Britain rule Afghanistan, any more than U.S. supersonic fighters can help defeat either the Taliban or drug smugglers there. After one catastrophic defeat and a couple of costly and fruitless victories, the British had to settle for indirect influence over Afghanistan during the last seventy years of their presence in the region.

Just as real military power is power that can be used, so real economic strength, from a geopolitical point of view, is strength that can be sustained. It is true that in the 1950s, military spending was a larger proportion of U.S. GDP (gross domestic product) than is now the case. But in the 1950s, the government had far fewer commitments to fund domestic programs, including not just those helping the poor, but the notorious "third rails" of middle-class entitlement: Social Security and Medicare.

Given these other commitments, the economic burden of a $400 billion defense budget is indeed substantial. And just as the American middle classes will not sacrifice these benefits to support imperial wars, nor will they, or the wealthy elites, pay higher taxes to support those wars. This pattern of imperial decline is hardly new. As many scholars of imperial China have suggested, several dynasties fell not because the Chinese economy got weaker or China's barbarian enemies stronger but because the Chinese local elites grew powerful enough to avoid paying the taxes that the state needed to pay its soldiers, repair its fortresses and canals, and buy allies among the neighboring nomadic peoples.

The bottom line is that even for an economic superpower like the United States, war is hideously expensive—and that goes not just for large-scale war but for war against small guerrilla forces as well, as in Iraq. By spring 2006, the direct cost of the Iraq War to the U.S. taxpayer already stood at more than $400 billion, with no end in sight.[10] Now, that's real money, even by American standards. The cost of the Iraq War, coupled with tax cuts, has pushed the budget deficit to record heights and greatly increased dependence on China (because the Chinese have been busily buying up America's increased debt) and general long-term economic vulnerability.

Meanwhile, terrorist and guerrilla wars cost our enemies very little. Kipling recognized this more than a hundred years ago, in his poem "Arithmetic on the Frontier."

A scrimmage in a border station
A canter down some dark defile

Two thousand pounds of education
Fall to a ten-rupee jezail. . . .

Strike hard who cares, shoot straight who can
The odds are on the cheaper man. . . .

With home-bred hordes the hillsides teem.
The troopships bring us one by one
At vast expense of time and steam,
To slay the Afridi where they run.
The "captives of our bow and spear"
are cheap, alas! as we are dear.[11]

The *jezail* (a crude Afghan musket) of today is the "improvised explosive device" (IED) being used against our troops in Iraq. And an Associated Press headline of March 13, 2006, said it all: "U.S. Military Spends Billions of Dollars to Defeat IEDs," which cost almost nothing to cobble together from old Iraqi artillery shells.

But the terrorist threat does more than change the military and financial equation. It fundamentally alters the terms on which U.S. power and strategy are calculated, and it does so in a way that makes the United States weaker, not stronger, than Britain was for most of the nineteenth century.

This is because the power to destroy states has lost much of its credibility, at least as far as the Muslim world is concerned. For the United States to destroy existing Muslim states is exactly what our extremist enemies want. We helped destroy the pro-Soviet Communist state in Afghanistan, and what did we get? A decade of anarchy, followed by the triumph of the Taliban and a safe haven for Al Qaeda. We destroyed the Baathist state in Iraq, and what did we get? A huge terrorist presence where none had existed before, and—as in Afghanistan under the Soviets—a training ground for jihadis from all over the Muslim world, who will now return to their own countries to spread revolution and terror there.

The British could credibly threaten to destroy states that refused to follow their wishes. We cannot. Even if Pakistan in the future abandons the war on terror, we can neither occupy Pakistan nor threaten to overthrow it as a state. We do not have the troops for the former, and the latter would simply hand it over to the extremists.

Even threats of economic pressure against countries like Pakistan have become a double-edged sword, for even a partly cooperative Pakistani state will be better than one that collapses completely, leaving a maelstrom of anarchy, a perfect breeding ground for terrorism, and possibly—the ultimate nightmare—Pakistan's nuclear weapons in the hands of terrorists.

But even short of such apocalyptic scenarios, we have to recognize that the terrorist threat means that detailed local cooperation is essential. Fighting terrorists and extremists is dependent on the cooperation of ordinary Muslims in many countries, and especially of Muslim policemen and security forces. The alliance of the administration of Pervez Musharraf in Pakistan with the United States in fighting terrorism will be pointless if in practice Pakistani moves to arrest terrorists are continually leaked to those terrorists by sympathizers in the Pakistani army and police.

We cannot do without the help of such Muslim forces; and to gain and keep their help, they have to be convinced that fighting against Al Qaeda is their duty as patriots: that it accords with the national interests, the national traditions, and the national pride of their respective countries. This applies especially, of course, to deeply patriotic forces like the Pakistani officer corps. In turn, this consideration puts severe limits on the employment of U.S. power. For crude exercises of that power—such as when U.S. forces attempt to strike at suspected Al Qaeda targets without informing the Musharraf government, which humiliates the Pakistani government before its own people and especially its own soldiers—will not really be a victory even if they do succeed in killing terrorist leaders on Pakistani soil. Such actions, on the contrary, risk swapping a limited tactical victory for a really serious strategic defeat.

Even with regard to non-Muslim great power rivals, the United States is often weaker than it seems. The combination of a huge trade deficit with China, a record budget deficit, and a negative savings rate has led the United States into a position of economic dependency on Beijing that Truman and Eisenhower would have regarded as virtually treasonable. It is true, of course, that at present this is a mutual dependency. China is equally dependent on an open American market for its exports of consumer goods. This is a kind of "Mexican standoff": China can threaten to kill the U.S. economy by no longer buying United States bonds and securities, and the United States can threaten to kill the Chinese economy by erecting tariff walls.

But according to the present terms of this standoff, the United States as global hegemon will lose whichever side weakens first. If in the years to come China develops its own huge middle class and no longer needs to export to the United States on such a scale, then what will America do when China dictates geopolitical terms in return for continuing to fund the U.S. consumer boom? On the other hand, if China experiences a political upheaval that brings its own economic boom to an end, Beijing will no longer be able to buy U.S. stocks and dollars, and the U.S. consumer boom will collapse—and with it, probably, even a limited willingness of U.S. taxpayers to go on paying the costs of empire.

Russia today is not nearly as strong as China on a global scale. As the United States is discovering, however, military and political strengths are not absolute, but depend to a considerable degree on location. Since the end of the Cold War, Moscow has no longer had either the ability or the desire to compete with the United States in Latin America, Africa, Southeast Asia, and Central Europe or even to a considerable degree in the Middle East. But Ukraine, the Caucasus, and Central Asia are different. There, many countries remain dependent on Russia economically. And in some countries like Ukraine, not just elite groups but much of the population continue to speak Russian, to identify with Moscow, and to want a close alliance with Russia.

The United States may urge NATO membership for Ukraine, but if the Russians in the east and south of Ukraine rebelled and demanded to join Russia, would Washington send in troops to crush them by force? Really? And could Washington do so, if for example the U.S. military was bogged down in another Middle Eastern quagmire like Iraq, was facing Islamist revolution in Saudi Arabia, or was in a military confrontation with China over Taiwan? And if the United States couldn't defend Ukrainian territorial integrity, would NATO's European members do so? (If you believe that, we have some Iraqi currency we'd like to sell you.)

NATO's statutory Article 5 guarantee to defend its members is permanent. But the present balance of political and economic strength in Eurasia is not forever, but in fact is changing before our eyes. However it changes, America will be expected to uphold those security commitments to which it has pledged its national word and its national honor through the signature of treaties like NATO. But for the United States to take on new security commitments without being sure of its ability or even its real willingness to fulfill them is neither honorable nor wise. As George Kennan remarked shortly before his death, "This expansion [of NATO] would make the founding fathers turn over in their graves. We have signed up to protect a whole series of countries even though we have neither the resources nor the intention to do so in any serious way."[12]

The Folly of Democratism

Because of the Iraqi quagmire, the budget deficit, and obvious military strain, the Pentagon is deeply worried about overstretch; and a certain awareness of limits on American power is growing among the wiser elements of the U.S. policy elites. Even in these circles, however, a widespread belief exists that in the former Soviet Union and in the Muslim world, America can compensate for these weaknesses by encouraging the spread of democracy.

This is a bipartisan faith, shared not just by neoconservatives and liberal hawks, but by a majority of the leaderships of both parties, by majorities in establishment think tanks like the Carnegie

Endowment and the Brookings Institution, and by much of the foreign policy bureaucracy. It is not a fantasy cooked up by the neoconservatives, but has deep roots in certain strands of the American
tradition. It is also often deeply and tragically mistaken.[13]

The element of classical tragedy lies in the fact that, in itself,
spreading democracy is a noble and worthwhile goal. A world in
which democracies are more widespread, more secure, and more
firmly anchored should indeed be part of the American legacy
to humanity that transcends U.S. global power and will endure for
millennia after that power has vanished.[14]

The errors lie in believing that the spread of democracy consists
of progress down a single known path to a fixed and preordained
goal; that this progress can and should be linked to the achievement of short- and medium-term American foreign policy goals;
and that true democrats in other countries should be expected to
invariably support those goals, even if they conflict with the national
interests of their own countries.[15]

The beliefs that democracy can be easily spread, that it can be
combined with free market economic reform, and that it will lead
to countries becoming peaceful and pro-American are expressed in
the National Security Strategy of 2006, a large proportion of which
is devoted to these themes.[16]

Insofar as this analysis is based on anything other than ideological faith, it draws almost exclusively on the history of Eastern
Europe during and after the fall of Communism. But as Francis
Fukuyama and others have now argued, the East European case is
unique and must not be universalized. One reason is that in Eastern Europe, nationalism was mobilized behind political and economic reform in a way that cannot be replicated elsewhere—least
of all in the Middle East, where much of Arab and Iranian nationalism is bitterly anti-American. East Europeans committed themselves to democracy and reform as a way of escaping the hated
influence of Moscow and fulfilling what they regarded as their historically mandated national destinies of joining the West. In East-

ern Europe, therefore, nationalism, a pro-American outlook, and support for democracy all went together.

Moreover, in Eastern Europe the push of nationalism was added to the tremendous pull of NATO and European Union membership, and the tremendous assistance of EU aid. This combination of nationalism, democracy, and material incentives is not one that can be replicated anywhere in the Muslim world with the exception of Turkey and conceivably the Palestinian territories. EU membership is assuredly not on offer for Egypt, Saudi Arabia, or Iran.

In the Muslim world, both spreading democracy and attracting support for U.S. policies will only be possible if enough Muslims think that this is not only in their personal interest, but also in their patriotic interest. Preaching democracy and freedom at them will be useless if they associate the adoption of Western-style democracy with national humiliation and the sacrifice of vital national interests. Once again, nationalism is critical.

The problem is that much Democratist thinking is linked to aspects of American culture that make it difficult for many Americans to understand other peoples' nationalisms. As noted, the tendency to identify America, and U.S. international interests, with righteousness can too easily lead to associating rival nations with unrighteousness.

This is especially true where these nations are ruled by nondemocratic systems that Americans instinctively see as illegitimate. And many of the subjects of those states may share this feeling. On the other hand, on foreign and security issues, those states may well enjoy the support of the great majority of their peoples—at least when it comes to a defense of national interests, and an angry rejection of foreign pressure.

Dismissing the views of other states because those states are not democratic can therefore easily become a dismissal of the views of their peoples too. This is the line that has been followed by much of the Israel lobby in the United States with regard to Muslim criticisms of Israeli policies and American backing for them—and it has had a disastrous effect on attitudes toward America in the Muslim world, including among many convinced Muslim democrats. The argument that the Palestinians, and the Arab countries in general, must develop democracy before Israel can be expected to negotiate with them is being used by pro-Israel hard-liners to try to defer a peace settlement in the Middle East indefinitely.[17]

Amid U.S. professions of a desire for democracy in the region, the opinions of the vast majority of Arabs concerning the Israeli-Palestinian conflict and U.S. strategy in the region have been treated by U.S. administrations, and much of our political class and media, with open contempt. As a result, not only can the United States be prevented from mobilizing nationalism to support democracy and pro-American feeling, but thanks to the Israeli-Palestinian conflict and the Iraq War, America has made enemies even of many local liberal forces who in other circumstances would have been natural allies, and who are in fact natural and essential allies in the struggle with Al Qaeda and the Sunni Islamist terrorists.

Thus because of the bitter criticism of the Iraq War by Al Jazeera and Al Arabiya, the Bush administration and much of the U.S. establishment and media have treated these Westernized and popular Arabic TV stations as enemies of America—and have continued to do so even after the Al Arabiya office in Baghdad was destroyed by Islamist terrorists, and five of its staff killed, because Al Arabiya had denounced terrorism and extremism. In other words, the United States is trying to spread democracy in the Middle East without even having, or trying to keep, the pro-Western liberals on its side. Does this meet the test of common sense on which ethical realism insists?[18]

Among neoconservatives and liberal hawks, the desire to spread democracy can also take a form that is explicitly dedicated to the weakening or even destruction of other states, even when these are by no means full-fledged enemies of America. This kind of thinking has been given a tremendous impetus by the way in which mass "democratic" movements (which were in fact mostly nationalist) helped destroy the Soviet Union. Thus in a piece urging a

tough U.S. strategy of confronting and weakening China, Max
Boot of the *Wall Street Journal* wrote,

> Beyond containment, deterrence, and economic integration lies a
> strategy that the British never employed against either Germany
> or Japan—internal subversion. Sorry, the polite euphemisms are
> "democracy promotion" and "human rights protection," but these
> amount to the same thing: The freer China becomes, the less power
> the Communist oligarchy will enjoy. The United States should aim
> to "Taiwanize" the mainland—to spread democracy through such
> steps as increased radio broadcasts and Internet postings. . . . In gen-
> eral, the U.S. government should elevate the issue of human rights
> in our dealings with China. The State Department wrote in its most
> recent human rights report that the Chinese government's "human
> rights record remained poor, and the Government continued to
> commit numerous and serious abuses." The U.S. government should
> do much more to publicize and denounce such abuses. We need to
> champion Chinese dissidents, intellectuals, and political prisoners,
> and help make them as famous as Andrei Sakharov, Václav Havel,
> and Lech Walesa.[19]

Is it surprising that faced with these views, not just the Communist
regime but many ordinary Chinese and Russians view the U.S.
preaching of democracy as part of a plan to weaken or even destroy
their countries? This attitude toward the world almost recalls that
of the French and Russian revolutionaries of the past, for whom
any state that did not embody their ideology could legitimately
be overthrown. But the French and Russian revolutionaries were
declared and savage enemies of the international political and economic order of their day. It is strange indeed to see leading U.S.
commentators, citizens of the greatest capitalist state and linchpin
of the present international order, taking a similar line.[20]

In terms of U.S. national interests, the argument for the spreading of democracy in the world is based on the idea of the "Democratic Peace": the belief, repeatedly stated by President Bush and
other officials, that "democracies don't fight other democracies."[21]
This has also been used by the administration and its supporters—

mostly after the event—as a key justification for the invasion of Iraq.[22] It is indeed true that established democracies don't fight one another, but only if very important other factors are either added to the equation or removed from it—which means in practice that it is not true as far as much of the world is concerned, and for the fore-seeable future.

The two elements that have to be included are those common to the world's developed democracies, and that do indeed contribute enormously to the fact that they are unlikely to fight one another. These include all the legal and civil institutions that we in the West think of as naturally accompanying democracy—but that are in fact absent from most quasi-democracies around the world. And they include prosperity, which both creates middle classes with a real commitment to democracy and spreads well-being through enough of the population that the masses accept being led by the middle classes, instead of turning to some variety or other of popu-list demagogue, as is increasingly the case in Latin America today.

The first element that has to be taken out of the mix—and can-not be—is, once again, nationalism, or some mixture of mutually hostile ethno-religious allegiances, as in Iraq. As Edward Mansfield and Jack Snyder have convincingly argued in their book, *Electing to Fight*, new and weak democracies are if anything more likely to fight one another than established autocracies, as new freedom allows the public expression of long-suppressed national griev-ances, and as these are then exploited by opportunist politicians.[23] The fall of Communism led to a whole row of such cases in the Balkans and the Caucasus: The Croat, Bosnian Muslim, Serbian, Albanian, Armenian, Azeribaijan, Georgian, and Abkhazian gov-ernments and movements that fought one another in the 1990s were elected and mostly genuinely popular. In an earlier era, the fall of the European empires led to similar conflicts in several of their former colonies.

In the Middle East, we have already seen electoral victory for radical Islamist forces in Iran, the Palestinian territories, and the Pashtun areas of Pakistan. To judge by recent limited elections in

Saudi Arabia and Egypt, radicals would also win free elections there if the authorities permitted them. In the long run, democracy is indeed necessary for progress and stability in the greater Middle East, and for the defeat of terrorism and extremism.

But moderate, nonaggressive, reasonably pro-Western democracies can only be established in the long run if the social, cultural, and institutional foundations for them are laid by successful economic development—and this is a generational process. What is more, there is no chance of Arab democratic feeling developing in a moderate and pro-Western direction unless the United States changes many of its existing policies in the Middle East, and shows a respect—a democratic respect—for the opinions of ordinary people in the region.

As the history of the Middle East and the world illustrates, Washingtonian Democratist orthodoxy is inadequate as a means of understanding the origins of conflict, and indeed the nature of political reality in much of the world. Even more striking, it is also a distorted way of understanding freedom—including freedom as it is perceived by most Americans, and by the American tradition.

The founding document on which the moral philosophy of America's approach to the world over the past sixty years was based is Roosevelt's famous "Four Freedoms" speech of 1941, setting out the great principles that inspired the Western allies during the Second World War. Those who haven't read them often assume that they must include the freedom to vote. Wrong. Democracy as such is nowhere mentioned. The Four Freedoms are freedom of speech and expression, freedom of worship, freedom from want, and freedom from fear.[24]

Of course, none of these freedoms can exist under a totalitarian state, but they can all exist under a moderately authoritarian one—as in several states of Europe before 1914. Freedom from want and freedom from fear both require states that respect their citizens, but are also strong enough to protect them.

These include the rule of law, a reasonably independent and efficient judiciary and police, a law-abiding, honest, and rational bureaucracy, and a population that enjoys basic rights of labor, movement, and free discussion. All of these rights can and often have existed in countries where the executive has been unelected. All of these things, however, also require that the state be strong enough to protect its citizens from outside aggression, internal rebellion, uncontrolled crime, and oppression and exploitation by predatory elites, including the state's own servants acting on their own account and for their own profit, like the police in so many countries.

This is something that the Americans of the past understood very well, and indeed ordinary Americans of today still know it in their bones when it comes to their own society. Thus the nineteenth-century American vice president and thinker John C. Calhoun declared that state power always needs "a sphere sufficiently large to protect the community against danger from without and violence and anarchy within. The residuum belongs to liberty. More cannot be safely or rightly allotted to it."[25]

The need for a return to Roosevelt's Four Freedoms as a basis for our thought about spreading freedom in the world is shown by the annual "Freedom in the World" survey by the congressionally funded, semiofficial U.S. organization Freedom House. These documents are treated by much of the media and political establishment almost as the equivalent of pronouncements by the Soviet Higher Party School. And like those pronouncements, many of Freedom House's ratings possess only a tangential relationship to reality.

What on earth, for example, are we to make of the fact that in 2006, Freedom House gave China its lowest mark, seven, for political freedom, and a six for civil liberty—barely different from the seven and seven it gave in 1972, in the depth of the dreadful Cultural Revolution?[26] Does Freedom House seriously think that ordinary Chinese are no freer today in real terms than at a time when their country was being swept by waves of monstrous totalitarian fanaticism, leading to the death, torture, and deportation of tens of millions of people? Is this the same country of which two *New York Times* headlines of March 12, 2006, read, "A Sharp Debate

Erupts in China over Ideologies" and "Film in China: Fantasy Trumps Controversy, Officially, but All Movies are Available One Way or Another?"

If challenged on this and similar idiocies, Freedom House officials tend to reply that they work on the basis of very narrow criteria, like free elections and private ownership of the media. But this is not an excuse—it is a confession. After all, many of the economic, social, and personal freedoms that Freedom House so rigorously ignores are precisely those that Americans themselves have always seen as integral to their free way of life and to the American Dream.

Too much of the Democratist ideology and its recommendations therefore fail the test not just of study but also of common sense. Too many American Democratists base their whole approach to the world on the assumption that they know how best to run countries of which they know nothing and whose languages they don't speak—countries that quite often they have never even visited! Would you hire a junior marketing executive with these credentials? For our part, we know perfectly well that we could not sell two plates of bean shoots in China or two sticks of kebab in Iran. We suspect, however, that most of those advocating Democratism in these countries could not sell even half a plate.

The Great Capitalist Peace

The Bush administration's National Security Strategy of 2006 contains one passage with which we are in complete agreement, and that could indeed form part of a manifesto for the Great Capitalist Peace:

> Relations with the most powerful countries in the world are central to our national security strategy. Our priority is pursuing American interests within cooperative relationships, particularly with our oldest and closest friends and allies. At the same time, we must seize the opportunity—unusual in historical terms—of an absence of

fundamental conflict between the great powers. Another priority, therefore, is preventing the reemergence of the great power rivalries that divided the world in previous eras. . . .

The struggle against militant Islamic radicalism is the great ideological conflict of the early years of the 21st Century and finds the great powers all on the same side—opposing the terrorists. This circumstance differs profoundly from the ideological struggles of the 20th century, which saw the great powers divided by ideology as well as by national interest.[27]

As a basis for strategy, this analysis and the spirit behind it are entirely correct. They are indeed just common sense, when the cities of America, Russia, India—and in the future probably China too—are all threatened with annihilation by Islamist terrorists seeking weapons of mass destruction.

But the strategy as actually followed in this regard by the Bush administration has contained two potentially disastrous flaws. The first is that, as we have already pointed out, the really important ideological struggle is the one taking place within the Muslim world. Ordinary Muslims therefore have to be convinced that the United States is not simply lining up all the non-Muslim great powers in an anti-Muslim alliance. Unfortunately, some neoconservatives and members of the Indian, Israeli, and Russian lobbies in the United States have publicly suggested just this.

To help win the struggle with Islamist extremism, it is above all Muslim states that have to be drawn into cooperative relationships. This is not only because it is the citizens of these states who are forming or sheltering extremist groups. It is also because, once again, national strength depends on location. Iran, Pakistan, and Saudi Arabia are not, of course, great powers on the world stage; but within their own region, they have great influence beyond their borders—not least in Afghanistan and Iraq, even in the midst of the U.S. military presence there. In the context of the war on terror, and as we will elaborate in the next chapter, it is these states that must be brought into the Great Capitalist Peace.

Russia, China, and India for their part do of course have a great importance in the war on terror, but it is a negative importance. Apart from help in the area of intelligence, the best way that they can serve success in this struggle is by keeping out of the way. That is to say, through not increasing Muslim anger by their treatment of Muslim minorities and neighbors, and by not drawing U.S. troops, money, and attention away from the war on terror. Unfortunately, Moscow, Delhi, and Beijing have all worsened wider Muslim feelings of persecution by their brutal treatment of Chechens, Kashmiris, and Uighurs.

Russia and China have also served to distract U.S. attention away from the terrorist threat. This was obvious before 9/11. In those years, too much of the U.S. foreign and security establishment, and the neoconservatives in particular, were concerned with rolling back Russian influence in the former Soviet Union, and debating a possible new Cold War with China. As Richard Clarke, Michael Scheuer, Rand Beers, and other former counterterrorism officials have documented, far too few of them were concerned with the threat from Islamist terrorism—even after these terrorists had already launched deadly attacks on U.S. targets in several countries, including one on the World Trade Center in New York.[28]

For the future, the capacity for distraction should be obvious. Just imagine what would happen to America's ability to fight in Afghanistan and Iraq, to contain Iran, or to threaten future extremist Muslim states if it has to fight China over Taiwan, or send an army to protect Ukraine against Russia. In the worst case, the outcome could be complete U.S. military withdrawal from the Middle East—one of Al Qaeda's key goals.

The authors of NSS 2006 may well be genuinely convinced that the United States is neither threatening the vital interests of Russia and China nor engaged in a new ideological struggle against their administrations. But viewed from Moscow and Beijing, things look very different—and to a degree, unfortunately, they are right. It is of course very good that the NSS contains statements about friendly relations among the great powers; but the impact of these statements is naturally diminished if those powers know perfectly well from reading the American newspapers that these statements were issued only after long and bitter wrangles with proponents of a much tougher line against Russia and China.

When it comes to the absence of ideological struggle among the great powers, the greater part of the NSS is dedicated to stating exactly the opposite. The entire document is centered on America's mission to spread "democracy" and "freedom" in the world, not by the force of America's example—there is not a word about that—but through "transformational diplomacy," a euphemism for a mixture of preaching, pressure, and subversion. Passage after passage declares that "tyranny" is evil, retrograde, doomed by history, and that wherever tyranny exists it will be the subject of American hostility.

Somewhat mildly in the NSS, but harshly in other U.S. official statements, and very harshly indeed in statements from Congress, from congressionally funded institutions like Freedom House, and from the U.S. media, it is made very clear that Russia and China are included among these "tyrannies." By this public pressure on Russia and China, America is throwing away precisely what the NSS quite rightly describes as one of the great gains for humanity of the end of the Cold War—the absence of ideological conflict among the major powers.

This is only a weaker and more indirect form of the "regime change" threat that has been made against Iraq, Iran, and other "rogue states." As has often been pointed out, this approach is incompatible with trying to negotiate compromises with such regimes—because if they think that America is going to destroy them in any case, they obviously have no incentive whatsoever to compromise if this involves lowering their defenses.

If there is one thing that ethical realism insists on, it is a capacity to distinguish clearly between different grades of evil, and to choose firmly between them. With all their faults, states like Russia, China, and Iran are in the context of history civilized forces, which guarantee a reasonably orderly and secure existence to their

THE GREAT CAPITALIST PEACE

peoples and accord them—with spectacular success in the case of China—the possibility of material and intellectual development.

More important from the point of view of the American people, the Russian and Chinese leaderships are not planning to launch an unprovoked attack aimed at destroying great Western cities and exterminating their populations—if only because this would bring their own economies down in ruins, and provide a dreadful precedent for future attacks against them. Nor, incidentally, are the more moderate and responsible elements of the Iranian leadership, like former president Akbar Hashemi Rafsanjani.

And if the present Iranian incumbent, Mahmoud Ahmadinejad, is really dreaming of this—why then, he can surely be deterred by the same U.S. nuclear deterrent that we used to deter the no less fanatical Joseph Stalin and Mao Tse-tung. And barely a decade after Mao Tse-tung was uttering his own bloodcurdling nuclear threats against America, the Nixon administration formed a quasi-alliance with his regime. Is it really true, then, that the United States simply cannot talk directly to the government of Iran unless it first surrenders on all key points of its foreign and security policy? The Iranian hostage crisis is now farther in the past than was the Chinese-American war in Korea when Nixon went to China. Is this episode to define U.S.-Iranian relations forever?

At the height of the Cold War, Eisenhower said that he did not really believe in all the talk of the Soviet leadership planning its own preventive strike, because "there is nothing they would ever do that might lead to the destruction of the Kremlin."[29] Why should we think that the rulers of Iran care less about their own great and ancient cities? What do the United States and Israel have nuclear deterrents for, after all, if they cannot be trusted to deter?

Even in the case of Iran, still more those of Russia and China, there can thus be no comparison between such states and the barbarity of Al Qaeda and its allies, the enemies of all order except their own totalitarian one, and of all human progress. Or to put it another way, with such states there is at least the possibility of a rational accommodation of interests that will also serve the wider ethical goal of peace and order in the world. With Al Qaeda, no such accommodation is possible. In rejecting demands that Russia both accept America's right to preach democracy to the world and fall into line behind specific U.S. policies, the Russian foreign minister, Sergei Lavrov, summed up the basis of Russian foreign policy as follows early in 2006:

> We are far from trying to impose our approaches on whomsoever. But it has to be realized that Russian authority, like authority in any democratic country, is accountable primarily to its own people and has to defend their interests. The present foreign policy course of the Russian leadership—for all the critical discussions of its particular aspects—enjoys broad support in the country. We regard this as one of the bases of the social consensus that has taken shape in our country—the key achievement of Russia's development in recent years.[30]

This statement may well lead to policies that are uncomfortable for America, policies that Washington should try by diplomatic means to change. Any minimally honest American, however, must surely recognize that these are not the words of a follower of Stalin or Hitler. They are words that could be spoken by the representative of any reasonably responsible modern state—the United States included. American leaders need to listen to such words and react accordingly.

In learning to distinguish between flawed but still basically civilized states like Russia and the real barbarians, Western policymakers might draw on a classical image. Ethical realists well understand the words about Roman civilization that the historian Tacitus put into the mouth of the British chieftain Calgacus before a battle with the Romans: "They make a desolation, and they call it peace." Tacitus had enough moral self-awareness to know that civilization could be cruel—crueler sometimes, and in some respects, than the barbarians that it fought. And yet Tacitus would never have doubted that in the final analysis Roman civilization with all its faults was better than barbarism; and if we have any honesty about our societies, the benefits we derive from them, and the threats to them, nor should we.

After the end of the Cold War, successive administrations—Democratic as well as Republican—have aimed at gaining a predominant influence over the world in general. That is fair enough, given America's economic weight, military strength, and important interests in every part of the world. It is also a program with which the mass of the American people would probably be broadly in agreement. The problem is that the administrations of Bill Clinton and George W. Bush have tried to do something more, something that by traditional historical standards is megalomaniac, aggressive, extremely dangerous, and above all far beyond America's strength. This is to gain predominant and even exclusive influence in every region of the world, including regions that are the traditional sphere of influence of powerful regional states. In the words of the historian Walter Russell Mead:

> In the 1990s, we came to the next stage [in the extension of U.S. claims to dominance]. The next stage would be a "global only" option, in which the U.S. would be entirely sovereign with no system of checks and balances and no accountability of our actions from anyone other than ourselves. . . . Current U.S. policies can be read as globalizing the same system of international relations which were established in Latin America in the 19th century. This cannot be seen as the basis for an alliance of equals.[31]

It should be absolutely clear by now that this strategy just isn't working, and that if America goes on attempting it, the result will be a degree of overstretch that will quickly destroy U.S. global leadership. America is certainly very strong, but it can't possibly be strong everywhere. If it tries to be, then sooner or later it will experience either a disastrous defeat, or an almost equally disastrous humiliation when some gimcrack local "ally" to whom America has recklessly promised help suddenly finds out in a crisis that America in fact has no help left to give.

We are certainly not arguing that America should pull out of any region of the world and simply hand it over to a local hegemon. This would be wrong, since after all the United States does have legitimate and important interests in many areas. What we are saying is that the United States should seek reasonable accommodations with other powers aimed at sharing influence and, above all, at preventing instability, state collapse, and the rise of extremism and terrorism.

The threat of terrorism to civilization provides a rallying cry and an organizing principle for the world's great states.[32] The deeper means of integrating them is the world capitalist economy. That is why we call our program the Great Capitalist Peace. This idea depends on America as global leader, and therefore ultimately upon a measure of American strength and will. It does not, however, require America to be an empire, or even the global hegemon. America will, of course, retain enough military power to defend its own vital interests, but it will take care not to threaten those of other regional powers, unless its primary interests are genuinely threatened.

The open collapse of Communism in the former Soviet empire, and its de facto collapse in China, has given us an unprecedented opportunity in this regard. True democracy has not conquered most of the world, but a belief in basic free market economics certainly has—even if not necessarily on the American model. As a result, elites in Russia, China, India, and most of the world's other major states are now judged by their populations according to their ability to make market economies work, and equally important, these elites have tremendous personal and group stakes in maintaining a working international market economy. The same is true of the American elites.

Of course, this doesn't mean that every country won't go on acting tough to maximize its own economic advantage in that market. But unless there is an outbreak of collective insanity, no major state elite has an interest in the kind of international crisis that would pull their own economic house down around their ears, and lead to their being overthrown by domestic unrest. Central tasks of U.S. strategy in the world therefore should be to make sure that these foreign elites and peoples go on believing that their vital interest lies in international peace and order; not threatening their interests or their pride in such a way that they may forget economics and return to atavistic and suicidal behavior; and through economic help and integration, giving as many new states and state elites as possible a stake in the international market and therefore in international order.

It may be objected that this kind of solution to the threat of conflict was advanced before the First World War, when it was argued that the leading European states had become so economically interdependent that they couldn't possibly fight one another—which proved not to be the case.[33] But most of the European rulers of that era were not bourgeois capitalists, as at present, but hereditary monarchs backed by old military aristocracies, who saw the justification for their continued existence as lying in war.[34] What's more, in those days struggles weren't just over national influence or advantage, but actual conquest of territory. With very rare exceptions like Taiwan, that is no longer the case. The Russian, Chinese, and other elites will fight to defend their really vital interests if necessary, but unlike their pre-1914 equivalents they show no evidence at all that they are actively looking for a fight.

Beyond the obvious economic incentives lying at the heart of the Great Capitalist Peace, a change in American thinking about the rest of the world is also necessary. Such a world will require due regard by other major states for the truly vital interests of the United States. But it will also require the United States to respect others' vital interests, and not to assume that the need for the mutual adjustment of such interests can somehow be swept away by the universal adoption of "democracy" and "freedom." On the contrary, good and productive relations between America and other countries are generally necessary before democracy can flourish overseas.

In assessing what are the truly vital and legitimate interests of other states, the United States must not, of course, simply acquiesce in whatever definitions the rulers of these states themselves put forward. But it must, through prudence, responsibility, understanding, and a decent respect to the opinions of mankind, use the same rough standards toward them that it has always applied to its own vital interests and those of its key allies. This is not just the foundation of any stable and consensual international order. It is also, after all, the ultimate test of any ethical system, as laid down by every great ethical preacher or philosopher from Jesus Christ to Immanuel Kant: Any set of legitimate rules must be "universifiable"—applicable not only to yourself and your friends, but to others as well.

These universal rules—ethical rules, but also realist ones—for an orderly and peaceful international society of civilized states include security against invasion and armed coercion; territorial integrity; basic national cohesion and internal order; governments in their immediate neighborhood that guarantee a reasonable level of order; and a reasonable degree of their own independence in national economic decision-making.

American idealism and power have only been able to survive because they have always in the end been combined with an iron adherence to these basic realist principles when it comes to the national interest. A stable and consensual order among the major states of the world requires that the United States also recognize such principles when followed by others. Democracy is not really the issue here. Without international peace and prosperity, and the defeat of Al Qaeda and its allies, democracy will not be able to develop anyway in most parts of the world.

Five

THE WAY FORWARD

The objective of foreign policy is relative and conditional: to bend, not break, the will of the other side as far as necessary in order to safeguard one's own vital interests without hurting those of the other side. The methods of foreign policy are relative and conditional: not to advance by destroying the obstacles in one's way, but to retreat before them, to maneuver around them, to soften and dissolve them slowly by means of persuasion, negotiation and pressure.[1]

—HANS MORGENTHAU

For reasons of space, it is impossible for us to produce a comprehensive set of policy prescriptions for all the myriad challenges confronting the United States in this new era. However, on the basis of the philosophy of ethical realism, we would like to make some concrete recommendations for strategy toward two key players on the international stage, Russia; and China; toward one key region, the Middle East; and toward one key theme, which we call developmental realism.[2] We have a duty to present this outline of the Great Capitalist Peace in some detail, because far too many contemporary foreign policy analysts set out fine-sounding visions but are studiously vague when it comes to drawing practical conclusions for policy from them.

The risks to America and the world in the absence of a consensual global order will be enormous. Admittedly, it seems highly unlikely that in the foreseeable future rivalry between America, Russia, China, Iran, and other major states could possibly lead to bloodshed on the scale of 1914–18 or 1939–45, or even a limited global struggle like the Cold War. But then, a clash between these powers would not have to assume such a scale in order to bring the present world economy down in ruins. As a European banker once remarked, if a civil war occurred in Ukraine with the West and Russia backing opposite sides, "you wouldn't be able to hold outside investment in Europe in a fishnet stocking, it would run away so fast."[3] The same would be true of East Asia if the United States and China fought even a limited war over Taiwan.

Given the extreme interdependence of the world's major economies, and the deep integration of production processes across the continents, it would be virtually impossible to prevent economic collapse in one region from spreading to all the rest.[4] As for what would happen to oil prices if the United States and Iran fought a war—well, that hardly needs to be described. Widespread economic chaos and misery would almost certainly bring a variety of extremist regimes to power in many parts of the world, as happened in the 1920s and 1930s. The danger is, of course, greatest in the Muslim world, where major states could suffer revolution and become in their turn exporters of terrorism and extremism. If this happens, or if terrorists succeed in attacking a city with weapons of mass destruction, then in retrospect contemporary differences between Washington, Moscow, and Beijing will surely seem petty by comparison.

This should be obvious already. It has been decades since Russians or Chinese have killed Americans even indirectly, or vice versa. On September 11, 2001, Islamist terrorists killed almost three thousand Americans. We know for a fact that they would kill millions if they could find the weapons to do so—and that they would do the same to Russians and Chinese as well. Do we have to suffer more 9/11s and more Beslans before our rulers recognize this? Yet at the start of 2006, there was widespread talk in the United States of a "new Cold War" with America on one side and a

Chinese-Russian axis on the other—with the shared threat of Islamist terrorism seemingly relegated to unimportance.[5]

Those Americans who call for making hostility to Russia and China a priority, or for accepting harsh rivalries between America and these powers as inevitable, do so on the basis of belief in a "unipolar world"—a world in which the United States dominates everywhere and makes all the key decisions in every region. While the American analysts and politicians who advocate this do not always talk, or even think, quite this clearly or starkly, this is what their strategy in fact involves.

We have already pointed out that this program is far beyond America's real strength, and far beyond the actual desire of most Americans. Indeed, if it were set out clearly to the electorate, they would without question turn it down flat. That is why the proponents of this program have had to disguise it in a variety of camouflages, from spreading democracy to the utterly false notion that by fighting others in their countries we are somehow discouraging them from attacking us in ours—when in fact we are encouraging them to take revenge on us.

But the unipolar world program is unrealistic not only because it is beyond America's strength and will, but because of the determination of other great nations to resist it. Chinese, Indians, and Iranians all regard themselves as heirs to a continual tradition of civilization and empire stretching back more than 2,500 years. For almost six hundred years, Russia has regarded itself as the heir of the Eastern Roman Empire and the leader of Orthodox Christendom. The French have a somewhat weaker and more diffuse version of the same historical self-image. Belief that they are poles of human civilization, power, and influence is hardwired into the mass consciousness of these countries. The United States may be first among equals, but there are other people sitting at the table.

To destroy this belief it would be necessary to destroy these countries. Even India, now being promoted by America as a key ally, does not see itself as subordinate to Washington. Rather, Indians see cooperation with the United States as a way of bringing forward the day when they will be a great power not only in Asia but on the global stage as well—and will, if necessary, be able to defy the United States with impunity if their vital interests demand this.

To fit these ambitions into the Great Capitalist Peace without conflict, the first step is for the United States to abandon its attempt to be dominant everywhere. Instead, it should seek to retain global leadership by remaining the only great power that is present everywhere, and therefore has an important say in what happens everywhere—a very different matter.[6]

The only region where the United States must continue jealously to guard its exclusive dominance is in Central America and the Caribbean, on its own borders. Elsewhere, its normal strategy should be to promote regional concerts of power, through which leading regional states will also be able to defend their interests, promote their influence, and seek to reconcile their differences.

This is, after all, what over the decades the United States has promoted with considerable success in Western and Central Europe, where the United States is influential but certainly not solely dominant. East and Southeast Asia are also increasingly home to a net of different regional organizations and informal business, trade, and financial networks, that may or may not include the United States and China but that tend to work against any single power achieving regional hegemony.[7]

This kind of regional concert should be the first U.S. strategy to serve its interests, preserve the orderly workings of capitalism, defuse disputes, and avoid conflicts. If—but only if—another state openly seeks to replace a regional concert with its own exclusive dominance, then the U.S. strategy should be what has been called "offshore balancing," lining up other rival regional states to oppose a new would-be regional hegemon hostile to vital U.S. interests.[8] If—and only if—that strategy fails to work should the United States reach for the option of sanctions, let alone war.

For by isolating countries from world markets, sanctions work directly against the logic of the Great Capitalist Peace. They help prevent the growth of middle classes with a cosmopolitan culture, a stake in the stability of the world economy, and a capacity for building and managing democracy at home. In other words, U.S. sanctions are usually exactly what reactionary and repressive regimes want. As a veteran Iranian analyst has written, "The increased competition and liberalization that would likely result from an opening of ties with the U.S. represent a threat to the interests [of much of the Iranian ruling elite]. From their perspective, Iran is now a closed party—their party—and the fewer who join in, the better."[9]

Efforts to promote successful and equitable economic development should be one of the two pillars of U.S. strategy in the Muslim world directed to preventing the growth of Al Qaeda and other extremist forces. The other should be genuine efforts to persuade as many Muslims and Muslim states as possible to struggle against Al Qaeda—without their necessarily allying with us or accepting our wider geopolitical or even regional agendas. And this means genuinely listening to Muslim opinion, not preaching democracy at them and then giving official U.S. approval to "experts" who declare that "the Arabs have never been very receptive to Western idealism. . . . But they fear and respect force."[10]

This also means doing everything possible to prevent the war with Islamist terrorism becoming, or becoming widely seen as, a war with Islam—for in that case, as George Bush himself has recognized, the war will be lost. We must respect Islam, and we must respect the expression of Islam in political movements just as we respect the right of American Christians to express their religious convictions through politics. The United States has already accepted the election of moderate Islamist governments in Turkey and Indonesia. We should make clear that we will also accept such governments elsewhere.

The sole requirement for U.S. cooperation with these Islamist movements should be their own willingness to denounce terrorism and genuinely work against it. We need to recall the anti-Soviet strategy recommended by the ADA and adopted by the Truman administration, that of allying with the "non-Communist left" against Communist totalitarianism and Soviet expansionism. In the early years of the Cold War, the United States did not demand that European socialists support American policy in Central America or East Asia, or sign up to America's form of capitalism.

The United States concentrated on the main enemy and the area where these groups were vitally important to America. And so the only test was whether these socialists were prepared to resist Soviet aggression and Communist subversion in Europe. Today, we cannot ask conservative Muslims, or indeed Muslims in general, to adopt stances toward Israel, attitudes toward women, and the separation of religion and state that go against their deepest convictions. We can and should demand that they forgo the use of force in seeking their objectives.[11]

If we keep this in mind, we can find allies throughout the Muslim world. For as a revolutionary ideological force, Al Qaeda and its allies threaten the states, the economies, the cultures, and the loyalties of the overwhelming majority of Muslims. Apart from the slaughter in Iraq, the Sunni Islamist extremists have also carried out terrorist attacks across the Muslim world that have killed hundreds of fellow Muslims. Their plan for the creation of a universal Muslim caliphate threatens all existing Muslim states. Their plan for Taliban-style Islamist government threatens existing societies and economies. And their extreme Wahabi theology is the product of a specific culture of the nomadic tribes of the Arabian desert that has long been alien even to the vast majority of conservative Sunni Muslims.

When the Wahabis of the tribe of Saud erupted out of the desert to seize Mecca and Medina at the end of the eighteenth century, the inhabitants of those great and ancient Islamic centers regarded them not as champions of Islam but as barbarian fanatics from the Dark Ages. That is also the private attitude of many conservative Pakistani Muslims toward the Taliban and their Pashtun tribal followers.

Opinion polls taken in the Muslim world in 2004–06 provide a clear indication of America's opportunity to exploit this anti-extremist feeling among Muslims. These polls demonstrated beyond doubt the truth of the following three propositions, of which only the first seems widely known in the United States:

They show that sizable majorities in most Muslim countries have at least some sympathy with Osama bin Laden, Al Qaeda, and their allies when it comes to fighting against what most Muslims see as unjust American domination of the Middle East.

However, they also show that when it comes to supporting Al Qaeda's goal of revolution within Muslim countries, the imposition of harshly fundamentalist laws in the manner of the Taliban, and the creation of a universal Islamic caliphate, these majorities turn into tiny minorities—even in Saudi Arabia. Large majorities in key Arab states combine strong hostility to U.S. policies with belief in democracy for their countries.[12]

Finally, more and more Muslims are becoming alienated from Islamist terrorism by the fact that this is now claiming large numbers of innocent Muslim civilian victims. Al Qaeda's number two, Ayman Al Zawahiri, recognized that the foul and murderous tactics of Abu Musab Al Zarqawi against the Shia in Iraq are creating just this blowback. In a message of July 2005, he diplomatically urged Zarqawi to desist:

> The Muslim masses . . . do not rally except against an outside occupying enemy, especially if the enemy is firstly Jewish, and secondly American. Therefore the Mujahed movement must avoid any action that the masses do not understand or approve. . . . You and your brothers must strive to have around you circles of support, assistance and co-operation, and through them, to advance until you achieve a consensus, entity, organization or association that represents all the honorable people of Iraq. . . .
>
> For that reason, many of your Muslim admirers among the common people are wondering about your attacks on the Shia. The sharpness of this questioning increases when the attacks are on one of their mosques. My opinion is that this matter won't be acceptable to the Muslim populace however much you try to explain it, and aversion to this will continue. . . .

I say to you that we are in a battle, and that more than half of this
battle is taking place on the battlefield of the media.[13]

We need to do everything possible to encourage such hostility to
Islamist terrorism among Muslims, and to diminish anti-American
attitudes. This means no more "wars of choice" like Iraq—and no
more demands for what a British diplomat has called pressure for
"ostentatious displays of submission" by Muslim states and parties,
and public support for everything the United States and Israel do.

Developmental Realism

A key aspect of the British Empire's own Great Capitalist Peace
strategy lay in advocating global free trade, as spreading economic
benefits widely made allies more likely to side with London, and
enemies more likely to acquiesce in its dominant global role. A
similar strategy was skillfully adopted by the Truman administration, which constructed the Bretton Woods economic system of
trade and aid that led to unprecedented post–World War II global
prosperity. However, the global free trade system is now in genuine
peril, with the Doha Round of World Trade Organization talks in
danger of derailing the multilateral free trade process. The Doha
Round, with its emphasis on agricultural liberalization, has been
nicknamed the "development round," as liberalizing this one sector
would do more to further prosperity in the developing world
(whose trade products are overwhelmingly agrarian) than any
other policy initiative. The refusal of the European Union in particular to significantly cut agricultural tariffs means that the whole
round of liberalization may fail. Such a blow would have profound
psychological and practical significance. There cannot be a Great
Capitalist Peace without the benefits of capitalism being spread farther afield. The WTO is the best way to do this. Its failure would be
catastrophic for the world as a whole.

The current free trade crisis threatens to snatch defeat from the jaws of Western victory in the ideological Cold War. As a result of Communism's collapse and its own experience, the vast majority of the developing world now accepts that some form of more or less regulated capitalism is their only way forward, that trade, not aid, is the most important route to economic progress, and that foreign direct investment, far more than the World Bank and the International Monetary Fund, is to be looked upon as the key to sustained economic growth. In other words, on the economic front, capitalism has for the moment won the ideological battle, with the East Asian capitalist model of trade-led capitalist development now strengthened by the immensely successful example of China.

This is what makes the continued evasions and obstructions over agricultural subsidies and other forms of protectionism by the European Union, the United States, and Japan so tragic. Having largely won over the developing world after decades of effort, and having persuaded these countries to undertake often desperately painful reforms, the United States and, to an even larger extent, the European Union, stand rightfully accused of having frittered away their own economic consensus which would have undoubtedly improved global economic conditions.[14] We can already see how this has contributed to the rise of anti-American populist nationalists in Latin America like Hugo Chávez of Venezuela. Given the terrorist and extremist threat in the Muslim world, the consequences of Western trade policies strangling economic growth in that region could be very much worse.

Under Truman and Eisenhower, America fostered the boom in free trade following World War II, and deserves great historical credit for the unprecedented global prosperity that followed. However, American attitudes toward free trade have always exhibited a certain Jekyll and Hyde quality; unfortunately in the waning years of the Bush administration it is the latter who seems to be on the prowl.

For example, American agricultural subsidies, which according to the Organization for Economic Cooperation and Development

(OECD) amounted to $20,000 a farm from 1999 to 2001, dwarf the $400 a year the average farmer in Nicaragua earns. Yet the United States blankly refused to discuss limiting agricultural subsidies while negotiating CAFTA, the Central American Free Trade Agreement, saying it would do so only at the multilateral WTO.[15] This hardly seems an advancement of free trade, or of prosperity and stability in a region that borders on the United States and is vital to American interests. Likewise American textile subsidies have done real damage to our vital ally Pakistan, where about 60 percent of the industrial workforce is clustered in this industry.[16]

By contrast, in the 1950s and 1960s, relatively open U.S. markets for the products of South Korea, Taiwan, and Thailand were critical to these countries' economic growth and to strengthening them against Communism. The Bush administration has proposed a Middle East free trade zone including the United States—but only by 2013, far too late to make an impact on immediate extremist threats. In 2004, the administration opposed legislation to open U.S. markets to Muslim allies in the war on terror.[17] Immediately after 9/11, the administration's trade representative (and later deputy secretary of state), Robert Zoellick, urged that trade liberalization be made a core part of the war on terror. Zoellick remains in the administration. Trade liberalization does not, or not nearly enough. There have been helpful bilateral trade deals with some smaller Muslim countries, but even these lack the generosity and vision of trade policies toward East and Southeast Asia in the first two decades of the Cold War.[18]

And now a new variant of the American protectionist strain has appeared: nationalist protectionism, or to put it more kindly, security protectionism. In 2005 Congress blocked the bid by CNOOC (a government-owned Chinese oil company) for America's Unocal—despite the fact that the great majority of Unocal's oil and gas reserves are outside America. In early 2006 came the ports hysteria.[19] Despite being a globally respected corporation, DP World, a ports operator owned by the pro-American government of Dubai, was pressured into not operating six East Coast ports, although the Coast Guard, customs, and immigration people would have remained wholly responsible for security. It is hard not to draw the conclusion that the only strike against DP World was that it is an Arab company. Such xenophobic nonsense is hardly likely to lead to the public diplomacy turnaround that America so desperately needs.

This is not to say that America does not have a far more open economy than most of the rest of the world. Indeed, of the Big Three established economic poles of power (Europe, Japan, the United States), and the new pole represented by China, it is consistently America that has the least protectionist trade policies.[20] But that is what makes the turn toward protectionism so disturbing and so counterproductive. American leadership means America has to set an example if it wants its advice to be followed. For there is little doubt that others, rightly or mostly wrongly, will use America's turn away from free trade to proclaim, "We are all sinners" in an effort to protect their own industries. For example, it is hopeless to ask Russia to throw its strategic industries open to foreign ownership, or China to drop its de facto import barriers, if the Congress is going to insist that whenever there is the slightest doubt, U.S. national interests and national security trump the workings of the market. Increased American protectionism must be fought now at all costs; it could well strangle the Great Capitalist Peace at birth.

By contrast with current U.S. trade practices, the Bush administration's Millennium Challenge Account (MCA) is an innovative way forward in terms of promoting economic prosperity. Compared with previous aid efforts, it is geared to help countries that help themselves—in other words, it rewards countries that carry out sensible economic reforms and practice good governance. This new approach is a reaction to the decidedly mixed record of U.S. and Western aid efforts over the past half century. Although there have been some notable successes, all too much of the money spent has been wasted or stolen, and in many cases has actually allowed rotten regimes to avoid carrying out vital reforms. Of the 111 countries for which data is available, 35 actually saw their per capita income shrink despite over four decades of development assistance. In other words, they were poorer in 2005 than they were in 1960.

Under the MCA, recipients will become eligible for aid by meeting minimum criteria based on performance indicators—including rule of law, control of corruption, and trade policy—that contribute to prosperity. The hope is that other developing countries, tempted by the carrot of American aid, will make the economic and social reforms necessary to qualify for that aid, thus helping themselves before they receive a penny. At its most ambitious, a virtuous economic cycle may develop, pulling a number of states out of the role of chronic beggars.

All of this is very sensible in theory. The problems with the MCA—and the partly related Middle East Partnership Initiative (MEPI)—are with some of the practice. In the first place, both programs are hopelessly underfunded. As of 2006, only $1.5 billion in new aid has been approved under the MCA—not sufficient to make a serious difference to even one large Muslim country. As to the MEPI, its funding verges on the comical. In 2005, Congress appropriated just $75 million (half of what President Bush requested) under this program—to help build political reform, economic reform, educational reform, and women's empowerment across the entire greater Middle East![21]

This was due to dreadfully shortsighted and mean-spirited congressional cuts, but also to the difficulty states have had in qualifying. As an essential part of the war on terror the United States needs to develop country-specific knowledge that will enable officials to make discriminating judgments about a country's governance and reform efforts. On the one hand, we need to avoid throwing money away on worthless regimes. On the other, however, the rules being enforced under the MCA and the MEPI are so strict that in the 1950s and early 1960s they would have prevented even South Korea and Taiwan from receiving aid—which seems ridiculous given the economic success they achieved with the help of U.S. aid.

Contrast this with the approach of the Truman and Eisenhower administrations. They were both obviously deeply committed to the defense and spread of democracy and the free market, but unlike too much of the American establishment of today, they understood that democracies and markets will never be stable if majorities of their citizens are unable to afford the basic necessities of life. Unlike their crudely triumphalist successors after the end of the Cold War, these men also had a deep sense of the fragility of democracies and market economies, for they had seen both fall like ninepins in the face of the Great Depression.

As a result of this perception, the Truman and Eisenhower administrations were committed to levels of aid that would be regarded as positively fabulous by politicians at the start of the twenty-first century. The Marshall Plan cost roughly $120 billion in 2006 dollars. Total U.S. aid to Europe (including separate programs for Greece and Turkey) came to almost $267 billion. These presidents and their supporters saw economic development as just as important in the struggle with Communism as both military power and the preaching of democracy.

And in a considerable number of countries around the world, U.S. aid played a critical part in developing economies and reducing economic misery. This was true not only in Western Europe with the Marshall Plan, but in East and Southeast Asia also. American aid and the development it stimulated were crucial to saving several of these countries from Communism. Too many Americans have become convinced that the overwhelming majority of aid during the Cold War was wasted. This is not the case. There was dreadful wastage, but the United States was also largely responsible for some magnificent economic successes. And in two Muslim states, Malaysia and Indonesia, the beneficial effects of past American aid continue to this day in helping these populations to resist the appeals of radical Islamism.

The Truman-Eisenhower generation was also rightly convinced that to work in the struggle against Communism, this development had to be reasonably equitable: that it had to embody real elements of social justice, and visibly spread the benefits of economic growth to the mass of the population. In consequence, the U.S. military government in Japan implemented radical land reforms, and the United States also insisted on land reform in South Korea and Taiwan as a condition of its aid to those countries.[22]

Unfortunately, since the end of the Cold War this aspect of development has been drowned by radical free market orthodoxies, with disastrous results for the establishment of stable democracy in Russia, Latin America, and elsewhere. We urgently need to revive this older and wiser approach as part of our struggle with revolutionary Islamist extremism—for like the Communists, these forces too gain much of their strength from appeals to feelings of economic injustice and deprivation.

The identification of the United States with blatantly unjust and unequal economic policies has had a terrible effect on American prestige in many countries, from Latin America to Russia to the Muslim world. This is especially damaging to the war on terror, because of the special place of ideas of justice and dignity among Muslim cultural values. As the mufti (senior Muslim cleric) of Egypt has stated, "In authentic Muslim perceptions, justice structures all vital spheres of human existence. Justice is an absolute concept in Islamic teachings and precedes other central notions such as freedom and solidarity."[23]

The need for visibly equitable development—what Benjamin Friedman, professor of political economy at Harvard, has called "moral growth"—is not merely necessary for the war on terror and the wider projection of U.S. influence.[24] Nor is thinking along these lines only the product of left-wing traditions. Drawing on a tradition stretching back to Aristotle—who declared that "where the middle class is large, there is least likely to be faction and dissention"[25]—both Edmund Burke and Thomas Jefferson believed that if a constitutional state is to flourish, the active participants in it must possess sufficient necessities of life to guarantee their attachment to the state and to basic political stability.

We cannot re-create Burke's English gentry or Jefferson's American yeoman farmers in Latin America or the Arab world. But if like Burke and Jefferson we want to lay the basis for stable and long-lasting constitutional states, then we can and must help to ensure that the actual or prospective voters in these countries enjoy a reasonably dignified life for themselves and their children.

This strategy needs to come in two parts. The first, as stated, is the promotion of policies and projects that will visibly benefit the majority of the population. The second, which overlaps with the first but is also distinct from it, is support for the growth of middle classes—who for a considerable time will form a minority in the countries concerned, but who are essential to the creation and even more important the stabilization of democracy.

The creation of middle classes, of course, requires overall economic growth, but more particularly it depends on the provision of reasonably easy access to loans for small businesses and for home ownership. This in turn requires the right kind of regional, national, and local banking systems, funded to a sufficient level. The lead international player in helping to develop such banks is the International Monetary Fund, but it will be able to do little without strong political and financial support from the United States and the other wealthy democracies. A valuable model for how to promote such middle-class development has been provided by EU strategies toward the former Communist states of Eastern Europe.

It is essential that such strategies be pursued consistently over decades, and not be subject to short-term changes as a result of Western domestic politics. For while stable and successful middle classes are an essential foundation of democracy, a range of disastrous historical experiences (worst of all, that of Weimar Germany) shows that middle classes who achieve a certain prosperity and status only to lose it again can be the most dangerous political group of all.[26]

For at its core, our trade and aid strategy is designed to help accomplish two seemingly contradictory foreign policy objectives, one conservative and one revolutionary. On the one hand, American-led increased global economic prosperity is an essential ingredient in the Great Capitalist Peace we hope to establish. If an increasing number of states are notably more prosperous, they are far more likely to want to protect the present global system, and will be increasingly immune to the siren songs of the barbarians like Al Qaeda who wish to destroy the present order.

On the other hand, capitalism is over time one of the most effective means ever created of wearing down authoritarian governments. A very few successful economies such as Singapore's have yet to evolve into democracies, but in the great majority of cases, from Taiwan to Spain, countries that have developed a successful free market economy have democratized as a result. The decentralization of economic decision-making supports the growth of civil society by creating a nongovernmental space, thus leading inevitably to the loss of full political control over the citizenry. In such a case authoritarian governments are eventually put at risk regardless of how they respond to economic liberalization. Furthermore, thanks to the emergence of successful middle classes with the culture, the experience, and the will to make democracy work, the resulting democracies have thereafter remained stable.

It should be clearly understood that we are definitely not advocating pouring massive amounts of aid into a wide range of countries around the world, irrespective of the nature of their governments. That would simply be a recipe for the kind of useless, scandalous waste characterized by U.S. aid to Mobutu's Zaire. Our approach would be ethical, but also toughly realist.

As during the Cold War, truly substantial amounts of development aid should be made available, but they should be directed not at the neediest countries, but at ones that meet two basic tests. The first is that these countries should be truly important to vital U.S. national interests. This obviously includes Muslim countries that are critical in the struggle against Islamist terrorism and radicalism, but it also means those Central American countries whose poverty threatens the United States with harmful drugs and illegal immigration—countries that have been shamefully neglected by the Bush administration in recent years. On the other hand—let us be brutally frank about this—it excludes most of non-Muslim sub-Saharan Africa, however great the human need of this region.

This region is also unfortunately excluded as a result of the second test, which is that the states concerned should be sufficiently honest and effective to absorb this aid effectively. We don't mean perfectly honest and effective, for if such a test had been applied during the Cold War, great U.S.-assistance success stories like South Korea and Taiwan, and lesser ones like Thailand and Malaysia, could never have occurred. But honest and effective enough that a reasonable proportion of aid will go to the purposes for which it has been given.

This second test would exclude a number of other states that would pass the strategic test for importance in the war on terror. Thus Nigeria, with its deep poverty, its vitally important role as a supplier of oil to the United States, and its huge population of increasingly radicalized Muslims, may well seem an obvious target for massive assistance. But there's no point. Under both military and democratic regimes, the Nigerian state elites have proved again and again that they are simply incapable of governing their country with even minimal honesty and efficiency, or of administering foreign aid without stealing the vast majority of it. The same goes for countries like Mali, and already failed states like Somalia. Such countries should, of course, continue to receive humanitarian aid to mitigate suffering, but not aid for development, or only small and highly controlled amounts.

The number of Muslim states that pass both these tests is actually rather small. The North African ones are clearly Europe's responsibility. The remainder include Jordan, a Syria that demonstrates some commitment to reform and international responsibility, Bangladesh, and a few of the Muslim states of West Africa and the Sahel. By far the largest and most important target, however, should be Pakistan. This country is in fact a perfect case for ethical and developmental realism. As repeated democratic failures have shown, Pakistan's dreadful problems are not amenable to solution by the shallow, short-term, and inexpensive nostrums of Democratism; they require profound, and very expensive, long-term commitments on the part of the United States.[27]

On the other hand, as recent growth figures (in 2005 Pakistan had the second-highest growth rate in all Asia) and infrastructural developments have shown, though the Pakistani state is deeply flawed, it is nonetheless still reasonably effective—at least as much, for example, as was South Korea in the 1950s. Despite considerable barriers to Pakistani exports to the United States, these have grown over the past three years by between 10 and 15 percent a year. As to Pakistan's own protectionist measures, the U.S. government in early 2006 criticized these, but also praised Pakistan for having "progressively and substantially reduced tariffs and liberalized imports" since 1998. As a result, U.S. exports to Pakistan have also increased steeply. In other words, this is a troubled country with a corrupt bureaucracy, but by no means a basket case.[28]

So far, however, U.S. assistance to this vital ally has once again been frankly inadequate. By the end of 2006, Pakistan will have received about $3.4 billion in U.S. aid since 9/11, which sounds like a lot but is, in fact, very small in comparison with Pakistan's needs and the size of its population, and given that almost half of this aid is not for economic development but is security-related.[29]

The biggest single focus of new aid should be the improvement of Pakistan's water infrastructure, especially in the area of conservation and reducing the present appalling degree of waste. Water shortages present the greatest future threat to the viability of Pakistan as a state and society. If present demographic and ecological trends continue, then in a few decades, Pakistan will have 250 million people living in a country much of which is as dry as the Sahara. In particular, given the dependence of much of Pakistan's agriculture on river-based irrigation, the melting of the Himalayan glaciers could face populations downstream with a literally existential challenge.

The second focus of aid to Pakistan should be helping to provide jobs. Improving Pakistan's educational system—especially for women—is important, but if this only produces unemployed and embittered graduates, the sole effect will be to increase Islamist radicalism. And since the ultimate reason for U.S. aid to Pakistan is not charitable but political, it must bring visible benefits to ordinary Pakistanis. As the leading regional expert, Stephen Philip Cohen, has written,

> The Pakistani people must see tangible evidence that the government's tilt in favor of the United States brings significant benefits to all socio-economic strata. Most aid is invisible to the average Pakistani, who cares little about debt relief or balance of payments problems. Without being obtrusive or boastful, the message should be that America is vitally concerned about Pakistani economic progress. . . . Specific projects in the arena of high technology, improving indigenous manufacturing, and research and development capabilities would demonstrate that a globally competitive Pakistan is in America's interest.[30]

Finally, aid should help turn Pakistan into a transport route for goods and energy between India and Europe, via Afghanistan and Central Asia. This is also essential if Afghanistan itself is to be stabilized and its population given any real alternative to the heroin trade. Ideally, this should also form part of an eventual deal with Iran, in which Tehran suspends its nuclear weapons program under strict conditions, and in return, the United States promotes Iran's full integration into the world economy and new regional transport and energy networks.[31]

Developmental Realism as a philosophy and a strategy is open to two main criticisms. The first is that it is impossible to ask Congress and the American people to pay for greatly increased development aid, especially given the present level of the budget deficit.

We don't agree. In the first place, if the United States had only kept out of the unnecessary disaster of Iraq, it would have had vastly more money to spend on generally vital aspects of the struggle against Al Qaeda and its allies. A tiny proportion of the funds poured into the bottomless pit of Iraq would be enough to radically transform key parts of the Pakistani economy.

Secondly, we do not think so poorly of the American people as this view suggests. In support of it, opinion surveys are often cited that show that most citizens think that the United States gives a vastly larger amount of international aid than is actually the case. Actually, the argument of these polls is the reverse. They show that the American people have been misled by their media and elites, but that in fact they would be prepared to give much more generously if the government appealed to them to do so.

All that Americans insist on—and they are absolutely right to do so—is that aid should also be in America's interest, and that it should stand a reasonable chance of achieving a reasonable proportion of the goals for which it is given. When reassured on these points, the American people gave very generously during the Cold War—and if the threat from Islamist extremism and terrorism to U.S. interests and lives is not comparable to that of Communism, then what has all the fuss been about these past five years?[32]

The second objection is that this approach to aid is somehow contrary to democratization. This is equally false. The ultimate goal of this and all economic development should be the creation of stable democracies. However, the two do not by nature accompany each other and should not be expected to do so in the short to medium term. It is obvious from history that while economic progress is essential to stable democracy, democracy as we now understand it is not essential to economic progress—for only a tiny minority of the fully economically developed states of the world were democracies when they achieved their critical economic breakthroughs.

In fact, we have very little idea of what might be a universal rule for the best and most successful relationship between political and economic progress, most probably because there isn't one. The search for such a rule is the present-day academic and bureaucratic equivalent of the medieval search for the Philosopher's Stone—with the difference that medieval alchemists did not expect to be supported with taxpayers' money. The truth is that the paths nations take to progress are extremely varied and extremely complicated. Over the past two hundred years, the countries that have achieved breakthroughs to developed status have had an amazingly wide range of political systems, from democratic America to oligarchical Britain to military dictatorship in South Korea. China in recent years has made immense capitalist progress under an ostensibly Communist one-party state that has adopted most of the previous economic program of its bitter enemies in Taiwan. You don't get much more complicated than that.

The test for development aid (as opposed to humanitarian aid to deal with the consequences of famine, epidemics, and natural disasters) should therefore be not democracy as such, but governance. However great their human needs, there is no point in shoveling aid into states like Nigeria, whose officials will simply steal it for themselves. But this test should not be seen as anti-democratic but pro-democratic, for most of the key criteria of good governance are also essential to expanding actual human freedom in a given society, and laying the basis for future real democracy.

The Greater Middle East: Need for a Regional Concert

We propose to treat the challenges presented by this region as one set of issues—and not in isolation, as is usually the case with policy debates. This is both because most of these issues are in fact intimately linked, and because a key part of our answer to them involves a concert of powers covering the region as a whole.

Thus the question of the Israeli-Arab peace process cannot be treated in isolation from relations with Iran, because the U.S. treatment of Hezbollah, the Lebanese Shia movement, as a "terrorist group" stems directly from Hezbollah's hostility to Israel. And in turn, American demands that Tehran break off support for Hezbollah are yet another stumbling block to successful negotiations between the United States and Iran on the Iranian nuclear program. Similarly, it makes little sense to conduct consultations with Iran about the future of Iraq while simultaneously taking a stand on Iran's nuclear program that is likely to make any wider agreements impossible and could lead to actual war between Washington and Tehran.

Our core strategy in the Middle East is therefore to promote a regional concert, sponsored by the United States, the European Union, and the other major world powers. This concert would allow the United States to go on exerting its influence and pursuing its key goals in the region while taking a step back from its present strategy of unilateral regional hegemony.[33] And among other things, a regional concert can at least help make more possible the creation of a just, stable, and lasting solution to the Israeli-Palestinian conflict. This in turn may make possible a basic Israeli dream, which is for Israel in some sense to be removed from the Middle East altogether and recognized as an integral part of the West.

Israeli-Palestinian Peace

We will begin with this last theme, not because it is the solution to everything else, as some naive leftists believe, but because it plays a part in everything else, from U.S. relations with Iran and Syria, through the propaganda and recruitment strategies of Al Qaeda and its allies, to the wider question of our own hopes of recruiting Muslims for the struggle against Al Qaeda.

Thus Ayman Al Zawahiri has been remarkably frank about Al Qaeda's need to exploit the Israeli-Palestinian conflict as a means of gaining support even from Muslims who do not identify with Al Qaeda's religious and political ideology:

The Muslim nation will not participate [in the jihad] unless the slogans of the Mujahideen are understood by the masses of the Muslim nation. The one slogan that has been well understood by the [Muslim] nation, and to which it has been responding for the past 50 years, is the call for jihad against Israel. The fact that must be acknowledged is that the issue of Palestine is the cause that has been firing up the feelings of the Muslim nation from Morocco to Indonesia for the past 50 years. In addition, it is a rallying point for all the Arabs, be they believers or non-believers.[34]

As we have remarked more than once in this book, Know Your Enemy. If Zawahiri is kind enough to tell us these things, we would do well to pay attention.[35]

Our strategy for a settlement of the Israeli-Palestinian conflict is unaffected by the electoral victory of the radical Palestinian group Hamas in early 2006, because frankly in the end we will have to negotiate with whomever the Palestinians elect, and there is no sense in demanding radical prior concessions before we even begin talks. If the British had done that vis-à-vis the IRA in the Northern Irish peace process, there would have been no peace process.

Our recommendations for a peace settlement are the following:[36]

The Palestinians must forfeit the right of refugee return to Israel, except for some very limited and symbolic cases of family reunification. The Palestinian refugees and their descendants must be compensated for their lost land and property at a level set by an international tribunal, and to an extent that will not only allow them to create prosperous and contented lives, but will also transform the economic prospects of the countries where they live: Jordan, Syria, Lebanon, and, of course, the Palestinian territories. Symbolic contributions to this compensation should be made by Israel and the United States, but the overwhelming share should be paid by the Europeans. They should commit themselves to this in advance, as an essential part of bringing about a settlement. If they object, they should be harshly and publicly reminded of Europe's historical responsibility for anti-Semitism, and therefore indirectly for the creation of the state of Israel and the Israeli-Palestinian conflict. The U.S. Congress will doubtless compensate Israel for the withdrawal of West Bank settlements. If peace is to be achieved, someone also has to fully compensate the Palestinians—and that can only be the Europeans.

The Palestinian Authority and all the major Arab states that have funded it must sign the settlement treaty, recognize the state of Israel within the borders agreed, and formally pledge not to support violence against Israel. For the sake of reciprocity, Israel should do the same as far as they are concerned. The treaty should be witnessed and guaranteed by all the members of the U.N. Security Council.

Israel must recognize an independent Palestinian state with full sovereign rights, subject to security guarantees acceptable to Israel included in a treaty between the two states. Legally, the border between the two states should take as a point of departure the 1967 boundaries, since only this formula can win international recognition for the treaty. In practice, Israel would annex the largest existing settlement blocs in the West Bank, including the great majority of Jewish settlers, in return for due compensation to the Palestinian state. However, the borders must be drawn in such a way as to make the Palestinian state contiguous, viable, with free access to the outside world, and covering the great majority of the land of the existing Palestinian territories. The capital of the Palestinian state should be in East Jerusalem, and there should be guaranteed and uninterrupted road and rail links between the West Bank and Gaza.

All the above initiatives must happen simultaneously. As the ultimate trade is land for peace, negotiations on both must occur in tandem. The details of the proposed territorial settlement must be worked out comprehensively in private. Only when all details have been agreed to should the settlement be made public.

More then a decade of negotiations have made obvious the failure of an incremental approach. The United States must commit itself to the outline of a final settlement, gain international support for it, and put pressure on both sides to agree.

This settlement must be comprehensive and final. It will not be open to renegotiation. If it is violated by either side, this should bring retaliation from the international community, along lines that should also be laid down in the treaty.

In conclusion, we would add the following. We have a great deal of sympathy for Israel's Kadima Party and much admiration for the pragmatism and moral courage of Prime Minister Ehud Olmert. At the same time, it needs to be stated clearly that a "settlement" that is unilaterally dictated by Israel, and that leaves the Palestinians in isolated patches of land surrounded by Israeli territory, is no settlement at all, and is not in the interests of the United States, the region, or Israel itself.[37]

For there is no real advantage to anybody in buying Israel what at best would be only a temporary breathing space. The point must be to gain for Israel legitimate recognition by the region, and thereby also to contribute to regional stability, with any rejectionist states firmly isolated, and Al Qaeda and its allies deprived of their ability to exploit this issue.

In this connection, we also strongly recommend that the U.S. administration immediately begin a strategy of putting pressure on the European Union to formally promise Israel and the Palestinian Authority that if they sign an internationally recognized settlement, they will be accepted into the EU accession process (something that Israel would already deserve if its economy alone were at issue). U.S. pressure on the European Union for this should be considerably stronger even than that exerted over the issue of Turkey's EU membership.

Of course, actual accession will depend on reforms that are in any case in the interests of the United States, the international community, and these countries themselves to introduce. Above all, the Israelis must grant full equality of citizenship to their Arab minority; and the Palestinians must move to create a genuine modern democratic state, and end their present rampant levels of cor-

ruption, maladministration, arbitrary rule, and political violence. It
is essential, however, that both states—and not just the Israelis—
be accepted as possible candidates for membership, because like it
or not, even after a settlement they are going to remain closely
intertwined.

Accession to the European Union would in a sense take both
countries out of the Middle East. Especially if combined with NATO
membership, it would give the Israelis tremendous added security
in terms of their identity and their economy. It would turn the
Palestinians from an oppressed foster child of the Muslim world
(and a pretty shamefully and hypocritically treated one at that,
as far as the behavior of many Muslim governments toward the
Palestinians is concerned) into the richest and most prestigious of
all the Arabs, and ambassadors of the Muslim world in the West.
This, by the way, is a role to which the Palestinians are already
entitled, since together with the Lebanese, they are by far the best
educated and economically dynamic of all the Arab peoples, with
the strongest intellectual and cultural presence in the West.

It may be objected that the Europeans would never agree.
Well, a secondary motivation for this strategy is precisely to take
some of the weight of responsibility—and blame—for the Israeli-
Palestinian imbroglio off the shoulders of the United States and place
it where, after all, it ultimately belongs historically. If the European
Union did in fact refuse to accept even the possibility of Israeli and
Palestinian membership, the Europeans would have demonstrated
their hypocrisy and irresponsibility toward the Middle East. And
European criticisms of U.S. policy would go very quiet for a while.

Containing Iraqi Civil War

And what of Iraq? Whatever the intentions of the administration,
these facts are not in dispute: The war in Iraq and the chaos that
has followed have greatly increased Iran's relative strength in the
region; severely overstretched the U.S. Army and National Guard
and diminished their ability to meet challenges elsewhere; cost

over $400 billion and counting by early 2006, despite the fatuous assertions by former deputy secretary of defense Paul Wolfowitz and others before the war that it would "pay for itself"; left anti-American firebrand Muqtada Al Sadr the possible kingmaker in the ruling Shia coalition; and been a recruiting boon for Islamist terrorist networks.

It is too late to establish anything like a successful democracy in Iraq that could act as a model and inspiration for others in the region. On the contrary, the task now is to prevent Iraqi civil war from spreading to the whole of the Middle East. American moves for a settlement of the Israeli-Palestinian conflict therefore should proceed in tandem with moves toward the creation of a U.S.-sponsored regional concert, beginning with a regional conference to discuss the future of Iraq.

This conference and concert should include states that do not now recognize one another diplomatically. Within the boundaries of these meetings, Americans and Iranians, Saudis and Israelis can meet and talk—which would naturally include informal talks not just about Iraq but also about the other issues of grave concern to the region. In this way, such a concert would be a step toward the creation of Richelieu's "community of reason" in what has been a most irrational part of the world.[38] The recent history of the Balkans is an object lesson in the importance of such regional concerts. Through NATO and the European Union, the United States had fostered such a concert in Western and Central Europe, which proved critical when America intervened in Bosnia in 1995 and Kosovo in 1999.

Much has been made of the fact that in both the Kosovo War and the second Iraq War, the United States lacked a mandate from the United Nations. But this misses the point almost completely. Of course, formal U.N. approval is desirable when possible, but equally, the United Nations will never be accepted as an absolutely binding force by America or any other major state. In most cases, the United Nations also has only a limited capacity to bring real power to bear in a particular region. A regional consensus is a quite different matter. As the Soviet Union demonstrated in its invasion of Afghanistan in 1979, and America has now conclusively proved by its invasion of Iraq in 2003, a state that invades another country in the face of an opposing regional consensus may or may not be acting illegally, but is certainly acting like a damned fool. For neighbors have an obvious and enormous capacity to affect the course of the resulting conflicts for good or ill. Thus in the case of Kosovo, the support or acquiescence of the major regional states in NATO's use of force—including, most important, all Kosovo's neighbors—meant that the conflict could be isolated and confined. In particular, it meant that Russian military aid could not reach the Serbs. The contrast with what happened to the Soviets in Afghanistan after 1979, or the Americans in Iraq after 2003, could hardly be starker. In both cases, the hostility of the regional states allowed a flood of volunteers, arms, and money to reach the insurgents.

In the case of the Middle East, we believe that such a concert is especially necessary for the following reasons.

First: America's present overt domination is bitterly unpopular in the region and serves as a principal recruiting tool for Al Qaeda. Given the unstable and violent nature of the region, any power attempting to exercise this kind of hegemony is also bound to be drawn into repeated wars—with potentially disastrous results for America's wider global leadership. It is highly desirable therefore that the United States take a step back, and seek both to limit its power and to veil it as far as possible behind that of regional states and regional agreements.[39]

Second: A regional concert is essential to containing the increased violence that is bound to occur in Iraq after the United States—inevitably—withdraws its troops from that country. The ultimate nightmare is not only that this conflict will turn into a full-scale Iraqi civil war between different factions of Shia, Sunnis, and Kurds, but that Turkey, Iran, Saudi Arabia, and other states will be drawn in to back their respective allies—like the Lebanese chaos of the 1970s and 1980s but on a much larger and grimmer scale, and with much more destabilizing consequences for the region.

Third: Such a regional approach can play an important role in fostering responsible behavior by Iran and Syria, and bringing these countries out of their present semi-isolation and into the Great Capitalist Peace. This too will reduce support for Palestinian extremists and make more likely the achievement of an Israeli-Palestinian settlement.

Fourth: The regional stability and regional economic links that would be promoted by such a concert are an indispensable basis for economic and social development in the short to medium term, and for successful democracy in the long term.

The first task of such a concert, however, would be to contain the Iraqi civil war. This must be through an agreement of all the regional states to respect Iraq's existing borders; to accept a federal framework for Iraq with guaranteed ethnic power-sharing at the center; and above all, not to arm opposing factions and risk a regional war. This agreement should be witnessed and guaranteed by the United States, the United Nations, the European Union, the Arab League, and the Organization of the Islamic Conference.

Many Americans and Israelis would, of course, view such a concert approach with horror, and for partly understandable reasons. But what is the real alternative? It must surely be obvious by now that the Bush administration has created a dreadful mess in Iraq; that it is proving incapable of controlling that mess; that the Iraqi political and security institutions the United States has set up are also failing; and that if things go on as they are, we will end up with a full-scale civil war, which may well turn into a regional war sucking in all the major neighboring states. And by invading and occupying Iraq, the United States by every ethical standard has taken responsibility for this country and its fate.

The biggest objections will probably be to the inclusion of Iran in this conference and this concert. But let's face it—powerful Iranian influence in Iraq is a fact. It is a fact that in early 2006 the Bush administration accepted by instructing the U.S. ambassador in Iraq, Zalmay Khalilzad, to begin talks with the Iranians on the subject of Iraq. This decision implicitly recognized that the U.S. goal now is not and cannot be to exclude Iranian influence, but only to make sure that it is exercised in a positive way that is not radically incompatible with American goals.[40]

On occasion, very much in private, sometimes after a few drinks, it is suggested by American and Israeli analysts that all this is quite unnecessary and that the United States should not worry about civil war in Iraq or regional war in the Middle East between Sunnis and Shia. On the contrary, these people say, we should encourage this, just as we encouraged the Iran-Iraq War in the 1980s. The reasoning is that such a conflict would probably last decades, would hopelessly split the Muslim world, and would tie down both Sunni and Shia extremists and prevent them from attacking Western targets.

To this a number of replies are possible. From a realist perspective, we can rightly say that such a conflict would probably lead to radical increases in oil prices and instability in oil markets, with severe effects on the world economy; that it might indeed lead to Shia revolt in the oilfields of Saudi Arabia, knocking the very bottom out of world oil supplies; that Al Qaeda is bound to benefit from such chaos in terms of recruitment; and that far from preventing anti-Western terrorism, it would probably encourage it, as Western states would inevitably be drawn in and would then be attacked by the other side. And if the past is anything to go by, the violent radicalization of huge numbers of Sunnis and Shia would inevitably sooner or later take an anti-Western form.

All of this is true, but none of it is our most important reason for opposing this kind of thinking. The chief reason we oppose it is that it is morally foul. If after everything American leaders have said about freedom, morality, and peace the United States were to adopt such a strategy, it would damn itself in the eyes of the world. This would be a repeat of the West's shameful acquiescence in Saddam Hussein's use of chemical weapons against the Kurds and Iranians in the 1980s, but on a much larger scale and with a far greater number of innocent casualties. As we have pointed out, among the key goals of U.S. strategy should be to leave behind an image of America that will influence the world in a positive direction for many years, centuries, and even millennia after American global power has vanished.

Dealing with Iran

Opening a place for Iran at this regional conference and concert on Iraq should be one element in the very slow process of establishing normal relations between the United States and the Islamic republic, and settling or at least containing the differences between them. Understand that we are not advocating a rapid "Grand Bargain" along the lines of Nixon and Kissinger's "opening to China." That would be naive, and looks absolutely impossible as long as the populist and anti-Semitic Mahmoud Ahmadinejad retains the Iranian presidency.

We had several chances to achieve this, and we threw them away. As Flynt Leverett (former director for Middle Eastern Affairs at the National Security Council) has revealed, the administration of Iran (then under more moderate and pragmatic leadership) made two credible offers of comprehensive talks—including on the nuclear issue—in 2001 and 2003, but they were simply brushed aside by the Bush administration.[41] The Clinton administration had previously failed to seize the opportunity presented by the election of the moderate reformist president Mohammed Khatami in 1997.

Today, given Ahmadinejad's character, other domestic political realities on both sides, and immense differences on various issues, such a Grand Bargain would be bound to fail. Nor are we advocating early formal U.S. diplomatic recognition of Iran, or the normalization of trade. Such moves must be carefully hoarded as U.S. bargaining chips, to be given up only in return for real and important Iranian concessions. On the other hand, it is just as utopian to dream like the Bush administration and many Democrats of a rapid transformation of Iran into a Western-style democracy and a willing supporter of U.S. strategy in the Middle East. The key to changing Iran internally and to producing Iranian cooperation and responsibility in its foreign and security policies is to adopt an incremental approach.

In consequence, it is simply idiotic to refuse to talk to Iran on specific issues of vital concern where there is in fact substantial room for agreement and mutual help. That applies to the civil war in Iraq, but also to the prevention of a Taliban victory and a new civil war in Afghanistan, and to cutting down the heroin trade from that country. After all, the Iranians played a critical role in preserving the Northern Alliance against the Taliban in the years before 9/11 (without which America's victory against the Taliban would have been infinitely more difficult and more costly) and as a result almost went to war with the Taliban in 1998. And over the past ten years Iran has lost more than 4,000 soldiers and police in clashes with heroin smugglers, and has the highest heroin addiction rate in the world.

To a considerable extent, talks on these issues can simply consist of putting more serious content into contacts that already exist. Thus the United States and Iran are both part of the semiformal International Contact Group on Afghanistan, and of international police bodies combating the drug trade. It is absurd that when the beginnings of contacts already exist on all these issues, U.S. diplomats who accidentally encounter Iranians at the U.N. or international conferences should have suddenly become obsessed with the view out the window or interesting patterns in the carpet.[42]

Enhancing such existing contacts can not only help with very real issues, it can also help build mutual confidence when it comes to the really big issues, which are potential Iranian support for terrorism and, still more pressingly, Iran's nuclear program. Is it really so unacceptable for American officials over a very private coffee on the fringes of these meetings to tell their Iranian counterparts that, of course, invasion and regime change are not options that anyone serious in Washington is thinking about? Or for the Iranians to reply that whatever the rantings of Ahmadinejad may suggest, Iran has absolutely no plans to reactivate its support for international terrorism as long as the United States does not attack Iran?

Instead of such a realist approach, we have what Reinhold Niebuhr accurately and searingly described concerning U.S. attitudes toward the Communist world in the early 1950s:

> Hatred disturbs all residual serenity of spirit and vindictiveness muddles every pool of sanity. In the present situation even the sanest of our statesmen have found it convenient to conform their policies to the public temper of fear and hatred which the most vulgar of our politicians have generated or exploited. Our foreign policy is thus threatened with a kind of apoplectic rigidity and inflexibility.[43]

From the late 1940s to the early 1970s, this "apoplectic rigidity" prevented the United States from opening direct contacts with Communist China. The result of this absence was two American disasters: the failure to predict the Chinese intervention in Korea in 1950 and the failure to understand the extent of the Chinese-Soviet split in the early 1960s, an understanding that would have made the U.S. intervention in Vietnam seem strategically unnecessary.

Today, by refusing to talk to the Iranians directly, we are failing to learn enough either about the real possibilities of cooperation with them, or about the points where they are genuinely implacable. In particular, if America wants to get anywhere on the nuclear issue, it just can't go on relying on EU, Swiss, or Russian intermediaries to carry its messages to Tehran, and then cursing the messengers when things go wrong. That is no way to build international respect and credibility.

A mixture of ignorance and irresponsible domestic political grandstanding led to the Bush administration's pinning itself publicly to a demand concerning Iran's nuclear program—complete and permanent termination of uranium enrichment—that no Iranian leader, government, or party can possibly accept.[44]

This has been made absolutely clear by every Iranian official from the supreme leader down, including all the chief reformers. Their stance appears to be backed by the great majority of ordinary Iranians, who see this demand (which is radically different from the approach of the United States and the West to India and Pakistan, let alone Israel) as yet another example of the "treaties of surrender" that for so long Western powers imposed on Iran. This mass sentiment emboldens the Iranian administration to run the risk of U.S. military attack, and the even greater likelihood of intensified international sanctions. Of course, its stance is strengthened still further by the well-founded belief that a military strike would probably fail, as would any plausible internationally agreed sanctions.[45]

The most that Iranian officials have suggested that they may accept is a small, limited, and strictly inspected enrichment program. This would not be sufficient to give them enough material for nuclear weapons—though it would give them the technology and the option to move to weaponization later if they decided to do so. This, of course, they claim not to want.

As in the case of Russia, we recommend therefore that the first task of U.S. policymakers should be to draw up a hierarchy of priorities with regard to Iran, and then on the basis of this to set a few clear goals—not the long laundry list to be found in the National Security Strategy of 2006.[46]

The two vital U.S. interests are the following:

First, to avoid Iran becoming once again a sponsor of international terrorism—something that it has not been since the Khobar Towers attack in Saudi Arabia in 1996 (which was a response to threats of regime change from Congress, according to veteran counterterrorism officials Richard Clarke and Steven Simon).[47] Preventing Tehran from taking this course is obviously a vital American interest, because if Iran encourages Hezbollah and other groups to launch a new international terrorist campaign, the terrorist threat would be drastically worsened (many Western terrorism experts regard Al Qaeda as amateurs compared with Hezbollah).

And there is another reason. If Iran were to be seen to sponsor major terrorist attacks on U.S. targets, any administration would probably feel it had no choice but to attack Iran. This could eventually lead to a full-scale war, with appallingly destructive effects on the world economy and the U.S. role in the Middle East. If this involved an actual U.S. invasion and occupation of Iran, the result would be an even more destructive version of the Vietnam War, with conscription bitterly dividing society, the armed forces becoming exhausted and demoralized, and U.S. global leadership destroyed. The only plausible reasons for Iran to adopt such a catastrophically risky policy as renewed international terrorism would be in response to a U.S. attack on Iran's nuclear facilities, or U.S. support for rebellion by groups within Iran.

As regards present Iranian policy, our test should be whether Iranian-backed groups like Hezbollah actually carry out terrorist attacks. The U.S. statement to Iran on Hezbollah should be the following:

We don't like Hezbollah, but we recognize that it is the democratic representative of the great majority of Lebanese Shia, and there's nothing we can or will do about that.

We also know that there is no point in the present circumstances in demanding that Hezbollah disarm. Even if we persuaded the Lebanese government to try to enforce this, the only result would be a new civil war and the return of Syrian domination—and in any case, to avoid just that disastrous possibility, Hezbollah in February 2006 actually signed an agreement with their old enemies, and Washington's old allies, the Lebanese Maronite Christians.[48]

We should tell Tehran that we know that since as the leader of the Shia of the world, Iran will inevitably have close ties to the Shia of Lebanon, you will have close ties to Hezbollah. What we insist on is that you use those links to persuade Hezbollah not to attack us, and not seriously to attack Israel (and we mean seriously—not the odd symbolic rocket fired into a field). If you don't, then we will punish you as far as it is in our power to do so.

Similarly, there is no point in demanding that Iran recognize Israel as a precondition of talks or agreements on other issues. Even for Iranians (a very great number) who are now openly indifferent to the fate of the Palestinians, the humiliation of this would be too great. Instead, we need to help the more moderate and responsible members of the Iranian establishment to do what they have in fact been trying to do already: to sideline the crazed Ahmadinejad on this issue, and return instead to Iran's eminently pragmatic stance: that it would accept any settlement that is accepted by the Palestinian people.[49]

Second, our other chief goal is obviously to prevent Iran from acquiring nuclear weapons. This is not because there is any serious prospect of Iran giving such weapons to terrorists. The risks of such a course would be simply too great. Israel has reportedly made it very clear to Iran in private that if Iran does acquire such weapons and there is a nuclear terrorist attack on Israel that can be even plausibly traced to an Iranian-backed group, then Israel will automatically launch a nuclear strike against Iran. The United States should make the same threat. In the event of a really dreadful terrorist attack on Israel or the United States, the likelihood is therefore that as a result Iran would cease to exist as an organized state and society.

A much greater threat, indeed a certainty, from Iranian nuclear weapons is that any hope that the Treaty on the Nonproliferation of Nuclear Weapons (the NPT) still had significance for stopping countries from going nuclear would be gone. In terms of nuclear weapons we really would be living in the jungle, with no norms and no agreed mechanism to pressure countries into accepting nonnuclear outcomes. In addition, the United States, the guarantor of last resort in the global order, would be seen to be helpless to stop a state from going nuclear. As a result, a significant proliferation of nuclear states around the world would not be very far away. For example, in the Middle East, Turkey, Saudi Arabia, and

Egypt are all prime candidates for quickly developing a nuclear weapons program after Iran crosses the threshold. It is unlikely that Israel would accept such an outcome with equanimity, especially as these new members of the nuclear club would have untried command and control systems. There would therefore be a very real possibility of a future regional conflict in the Middle East between countries with nuclear weapons.

As a result, the two chief U.S. policy goals regarding Iran should be the following:

In the long term, starting with the creation of a regional concert, to integrate Iran into the Great Capitalist Peace in a way that will make Iranians see the possession of nuclear weapons as just as irrelevant to their real national needs as do Brazilians, South Africans, or other nations that could easily develop nuclear weapons but have chosen not to do so. To bring this about will also involve beginning with informal U.S. security guarantees, and eventually building up to formal and public ones.

In the short to medium term, verifiably to freeze Iranian enrichment and other nuclear capabilities well short of weaponization (expert assessments on the time lag between limited enrichment and full weaponization vary from eighteen months to about three years). This time lag should be sufficient for the United States and the international community to receive sufficient warning of Iran's moves and to respond accordingly.

This international response should be agreed in advance by a public treaty signed by the members of the U.N. Security Council, the G8 (Group of Eight), and other appropriate international organizations. We have to stop this endless dance with the European Union, Russia, and China over the issue of enrichment and possible sanctions—it is getting us nowhere, and probably never will, since the Russians and Chinese have a much better appreciation of Iranian political realities than do U.S. leaders. Part of our problem also stems from the fact that as in so many cases, we have drawn a red line that everyone suspects will prove in a crisis not to be red at all, but a delicate shade of pink.

We need to draw a genuine, credible, and enforceable red line, and stick to it. And that red line must be moves to weaponization. Here, we have a good basis on which to bind the Iranians into an agreement, simply by taking them at their word, or diplomatically saying that we do, when they say that they do not want weapons and that their program is for peaceful purposes only. And the truth does in fact seem to be that Tehran does not want weapons now, but rather the option of developing them if necessary at some point in the future.

All the existing major powers of the world, for their part, say that they are strongly opposed to Iran ever gaining nuclear weapons, and we can believe them. The last thing that the other existing nuclear powers want is to expand their exclusive club and thereby diminish their own prestige. In addition, all are more or less threatened by Islamist terrorism, and are well aware that if Pakistan is followed into the nuclear club by Iran, then Saudi Arabia, Turkey, and so on, then the chances that sooner or later terrorists will get their hands on such weapons or materials will be vastly increased.

So we have every basis to go to the other major powers and say, We will go back to the letter of the NPT and allow strictly limited and controlled Iranian enrichment if you will sign a binding international agreement setting out in public, in detail and in advance, what you and the other signatory nations will do if Iran breaks its word and does indeed weaponize. These threats should include breaking off diplomatic relations, removing Iran from all international organizations, ending outside investment, imposing a full trade embargo, ending—as far as possible—all international flights to Iran, and inspecting all transport headed to that country.

As far as Russia is concerned, the United States should offer one additional incentive to sign this, and add a very serious threat. The incentive should be that Russia could be allowed to boost its international prestige (and of course the domestic image of the administration of President Vladimir Putin) by taking the diplomatic lead in this matter. The resulting international agreement could be signed in Moscow and entitled something like "the Moscow Declaration."

The threat would be that the United States would make Russia's adherence to its word on this question the top determinant of future U.S.-Russian relations. If Iran weaponized and Russia failed to respond as promised, the United States would retaliate across the whole range of relations, from trade links to NATO expansion. We would have publicly nailed Russia and other countries to this agreement, and we would publicly nail their hides to a barn door if they broke their word.

This approach must also, of course, involve the public abandonment of "regime change" in Iran as a policy. For this threat is utterly counterproductive from both points of view. It is diametrically opposed to President Theodore Roosevelt's advice to speak softly and carry a big stick. Shouted at the top of Washington's collective voice, it infuriates the Iranian authorities and makes it even more difficult for them to agree to any compromise. And yet, given Ahmadinejad's popularity and the overwhelming opposition of most Iranians to U.S. interference in Iran, we should be well aware that our stick is in actual fact a very small one. Certainly any U.S. money given to Iranian opposition groups only discredits those groups and makes them greater targets not just for official reprisals but for mass contempt as well.[50]

All this may appear unsatisfactory, but ethical realism demands first that we courageously face up to our real alternatives and choose accordingly, and second, that if our choice is for war, that we have studied the real probable costs and the real likelihood of success. In the case of an attack on Iran's nuclear facilities, the costs to U.S. interests would almost certainly be immense, and the gain might be no more than to retard Iran's nuclear program by a few years—something that we can achieve by diplomacy—while making Iran even more determined eventually to make nuclear weapons.

Consider the following: Having learned from the Israeli air strike on the Iraqi nuclear plant at Osirak in 1981, the Iranians have dispersed their nuclear program to approximately two hundred facilities (and our intelligence is bound to be less than perfect), buried many of them underground, duplicated sites, and shielded others by placing them in high-density urban areas, ruthlessly using their own people as human shields. As such, it is highly unlikely that an American or Israeli air strike could take out the program cleanly, or in its entirety. It would certainly set Iran's efforts to acquire nuclear weapons back, but at a calamitous price. With American ground troops not an option (given the size of Iran, the overstretched military, and the Iranian people's likely overwhelming support for resistance against an American invasion), from a military point of view it has become either a case of advocating bombing or eschewing the military card altogether.

In terms of public diplomacy the likely significant civilian casualties of even a limited U.S. air strike, broadcast continually over the global twenty-four-hour news cycle, would gravely further harm America's image in the rest of the world. For instance, it is hard to see, even for the most rabid neoconservative, how administration-led efforts to democratize the Middle East could survive a bombing campaign.

Given Iran's strong ties to the dominant Shia factions in Iraq (and especially to Muqtada Al Sadr and his Mahdi Army), there is a strong possibility that unrest in southern Iraq would get entirely out of control; at a minimum it would rival the unrest in the Sunni Triangle.[51] In February 2006 Al Sadr declared, "If neighboring Islamic countries, including Iran, become the target of [American] attacks, we will support them. The Mahdi Army is beyond the Iraqi Army. It was established to defend Islam."[52]

American terrorism experts have warned that Iran would retaliate against an attack by reactivating international terrorism against U.S. and allied targets, using both its own agents and Hezbollah. The presence of a large Shia minority in Saudi Arabia—concentrated in the oilfields region—means that Iran would also have a strong capacity to hit at Saudi targets, including, oil production.[53]

Another price of the bombing campaign would be Iran's likely efforts to make the West pay a significant economic price, either by merely threatening to withhold oil from the market (causing a spike in the price), or in endeavoring to block the Strait of Hormuz, if only for a brief time. As Europe is entirely dependent on oil from the Persian Gulf (and as America is entirely dependent on European foreign direct investment), Iran could make the West pay a fearful economic price for such a campaign. And all this for a military option unlikely to do more than retard Iran's nuclear program.[54] Such an attack would therefore radically violate the principle of prudence, which is first among the virtues set forth by ethical realism.

A couple of last thoughts on Iran itself: As with Russia and other problematic states, we have to get away from the idea that "democracy" is some kind of magic key that will somehow spirit away serious disputes between us. Most unfortunately, in the second round of the Iranian presidential elections of 2005 Ahmadinejad won fair and square against Rafsanjani, the more moderate establishment candidate. As for the liberal candidate—the only one regarded by the West as "democratic"—he came in fifth. Yes, Ahmadinejad was elected chiefly on an anti-corruption and anti-elitist platform—but to put it mildly, he didn't exactly disguise his hard-line religiously inflected nationalism either.[55]

And this reflects a historical pattern. In Iran as in so many other formerly colonized or semicolonized countries, the very beginnings of mass democratic politics (in Iran, in the 1890s) were inextricably linked to the emergence of modern nationalism, and of nationalist protest against domination and humiliation by Westerners.[56]

When it comes to the relationship between anti-elitism and nationalism—and so many other issues—Americans should draw more lessons from their own experience. We all know that one of the key ways in which poor but respectable middle-class Americans in the heartland distinguish themselves from richer, more cosmopolitan, and more liberal Americans in the cities is to think of themselves as tougher and more patriotic, and of the liberal elites as weak and possibly even treacherous.[57] Why do we think it is any different in the heartlands of Iran, or Russia, or China? Why do we think this kind of attitude could somehow be magicked away if we could only broadcast American propaganda into every home? Don't we remember what happened when the liberal British *Guardian* newspaper advised the people of Ohio to vote against George Bush?[58]

Finally, we have to understand something special about the Iranian state system, which was summed up well by Gary Sick of Columbia University, a veteran negotiator with the Iranians. He said that a critical mistake is to believe that the Iranian political classes are playing American football, when in fact they are playing a kind of chess, without conclusive winners and losers, but with agreed rules that are generally observed by the players.[59] If we want to gradually strengthen responsible elements and produce positive results in Iran, we have to learn to play a long game according to Iranian rules—not fantasize about changing the rules and sweeping the board.

Russia and the Former Soviet Union

In order to understand the thoroughly distorted picture that most Americans receive of events in the former Soviet Union, and Russia's role in them, it is worth comparing the media response to two recent Ukrainian elections. In November 2004, supporters of the government candidate, Prime Minister Viktor Yanukovich, who had the backing of Moscow, initially rigged the presidential elections (or at least, rigged them to a greater and more open extent than the other side). This result was overturned by massive public protests, dubbed the "Orange Revolution," which led to the election of the "pro-Western candidate," Viktor Yushchenko.

The Orange Revolution was intensively covered by the media, and praised and analyzed in countless commentaries, including numerous ones in the leading U.S. newspapers. However, sixteen months later, in March 2006, free and fair, internationally observed Ukrainian parliamentary elections led to Yanukovich's party winning a plurality of the vote.[60]

A central reason for this was that in the meantime, the chief parties of the Orange coalition and their business backers had turned on one another, economic growth—which had been proceeding very well under Mr. Yanukovich's corrupt but quite effective premiership—had plummeted, and the West, after all its declarations of moral support, had done nothing practical to help Ukraine.[61] The response of the U.S. media to the second set of elections? A bare minimum of reporting, and very little commentary and analysis. Once again, there seems to be a widespread feeling that democracy is really only worth supporting, or even reporting, if it produces results that we like.

As a result of this kind of slanted coverage, too many Americans—including policymakers—are completely unaware that Russia's continued power and influence in the former Soviet Union is not simply due to "Russian imperialism" and Russian pressure on its neighbors. In several countries, close ties to Russia are supported by majorities or large minorities of the population.[62] These ties are cemented both by old historical, cultural, linguistic, and ethnic affinities, and by close trade and economic links, including freedom to work in Russia—while freedom to work in the West is, of course, denied by Western states.[63]

This is not to say that the United States does not have genuine and serious differences with the administration of President Putin—for example, when it comes to the nature of Russia's relations with Iran. And there may be times in the future when the United States will have to punish Moscow very heavily indeed over this. There are also important U.S. interests in the former Soviet Union that will have to be maintained against Russia, and there will have to be red lines against certain kinds of Russian external behavior, including military pressure on its neighbors and crude attempts to interfere in their internal affairs. It goes without saying that the other countries of the former Soviet Union must remain open to outside trade and investment.

Ethical realism, however, calls upon us to draw genuine, realistic lines about what matters and what does not in terms of American relations with the other great powers. If the U.S. establishment line toward Russia remains as unrealistic, hostile, and ambitious as it is today, then chronic tension, and even clashes, between Moscow and Washington are inevitable. For if the United States gratuitously attacks Russian vital interests in one area, Russia will certainly retaliate against U.S. vital interests in others.[64]

In attacking Putin, Western spokesmen are not successfully appealing to ordinary Russians; on the contrary they are infuriating them. Like many other previous polls, a survey of March 2006 by the independent Levada polling organization showed 72 percent of Russians mostly approving Putin's overall policies and record in office, as opposed to 26 percent mostly condemning them. According to the same organization, at the same date, Putin's party, United Russia, had the support of 41 percent of the population. Communist and nationalist parties had a combined total of 37 percent. The total of the parties that the American establishment and media usually call "democratic" was 7 percent—rather far from a democratic majority of the electorate.[65]

You don't get much clearer results than that. And most of the reason for Putin's continued popularity is not that he has brainwashed the population. As the *Financial Times* wrote, describing the difference between Russia in 2006 and when it first joined the G8 nine years before, during the period of Boris Yeltsin,

> Russia in 1997 was chaotic, struggling to pay wages for millions, months away from a humiliating debt default and financial crisis. Russia today is firmly controlled from the center, in its eighth year of robust economic growth and displaying a self-confidence not seen since the 1970s. . . . The economy grew 6.4 per cent in 2005, down only slightly from the previous six year average of 6.7 per cent. Real wages increased 9.8 per cent.[66]

Moreover, the basic attitudes toward the state, society, and Russia's national interests reflected by Putin's policies have been held by the great majority of ordinary Russians throughout the post-Soviet period—including in the time of Yeltsin.[67] So while Putin will almost certainly step down as president in 2008, most of his key policies will probably be continued by his successor—with the support of a large majority of Russians. The U.S. debate has focused on the character, the ambitions, and—often—the alleged wickedness of Putin and his administration. But these are temporary phenomena. The Russian nation, its views, and its interests by contrast are a reality with which U.S. policy will have to deal for all foreseeable time.

Unfortunately, most of the leadership of both U.S. political parties are far from recognizing these realities. Thus in 2005, a bipartisan group of senators led by John McCain and Joseph Lieberman passed a resolution calling for Russia to be expelled from the Group of Eight for "backsliding" from democracy. It also demanded that Russia begin negotiations with "moderate Chechen separatists." This is a demand that the Senate would never dream of making to Turkey concerning its Kurdish separatists, or India concerning its Kashmiri ones, if only because any such demand would lead to the automatic collapse of American relations with these countries.

In their press release, Senator McCain accused Putin of "reasserting the Kremlin's old-style central control" (as if Putin possesses or could possibly possess anything resembling the power of the old Soviet Communist Party leadership). Senator Lieberman said that the resolution would "make a strong show of support for Russia's democrats"—unaware of or indifferent to the fact that the great majority of the Russian electorate would reject this Senate resolution with anger and contempt.

Instead of preaching democracy to the Russians while openly despising their opinions, we should work out what primary interests America has vis-à-vis Russia and the states surrounding it, make those interests crystal clear to the Kremlin, and work to reach consensus with them over these issues whenever possible, but also be prepared to exert serious pressure when necessary.[68] This will require accommodating Moscow when it comes to issues that are of lesser interest to us, but of primary interest to Russia. All the while, the long-term goal should be to draw the Russians into the Great Capitalist Peace as a great power stakeholder in a stable world order.

There is no reason to turn these limited disputes into new versions of the Cold War, or to infuse the American side in each of them with apocalyptic moral righteousness. In all too many cases, Russia is doing pretty much exactly what the United States has done and continues to do in several parts of the world, and especially in its old sphere of influence in Central America. Russia has been fiercely criticized by U.S. officials and politicians for using its energy reserves as a means of geopolitical influence—but wasn't it Dean Acheson who said that "American oil operations are, for all practical purposes, instruments of our foreign policy towards countries"?[69]

American officials like to attribute all legal and moral right in the ethnic conflicts of the southern Caucasus to the anti-Russian side. Yet this makes neither moral nor strategic sense; there is not an abundance of virtue on any side in the Caucasus. We should remember the melancholy example of the Soviets, who in the 1970s and early 1980s gratuitously infuriated the West, exhausted themselves, and helped destroy their empire by backing various savage, corrupt, chauvinist states and parties in the Horn of Africa and elsewhere if these claimed to be "socialist" and anti-American. Let's not follow their example by backing similar forces in the former Soviet Union as long as they claim to be "democratic" and anti-Russian.

Above all, relations with Russia are a classic example of the need for U.S. policymakers to distinguish between vital and secondary interests in dealing with other countries, and to establish genuine priorities accordingly. Just as with Iran and other powers, the United States should not have ten priorities for dealing with

Russia—such a laundry list, with each item dependent on solving all the others, is a sure recipe for estrangement. At the moment, U.S. officials claim to have so many "priorities" in dealing with Moscow that the very word loses its meaning.

In our view, the United States has only four vital interests in the former Soviet Union, of which three are also in Russia's vital interest. In order, these are the following:

First, to keep Russian weapons and materials of mass destruction out of the hands of terrorists, and to persuade Russia to prevent potentially dangerous countries like Iran from acquiring such weapons. (In fact, this could almost be said to be the only truly vital U.S. interest in this region, since it is the only issue that directly threatens the American homeland and the lives of large numbers of Americans.) This means, among other things, much stronger support and funding for the bipartisan Nunn-Lugar program designed to enhance the security of Russian nuclear, chemical, and biological sites.[70]

Second, together with Russia, to help prevent Islamist revolution and the creation of safe havens for Islamist terrorists in the Muslim regions of Central Asia and the Caucasus—something that is a very real danger, as the corrupt and oppressive regimes of Uzbekistan and other post-Soviet states crumble.[71]

Third, to preserve reasonably open international access to the energy reserves of Central Asia and the Caucasus (though the United States should work over the long term to make this a less vital interest, by reducing energy consumption and dependence on imported oil, for both environmental and security reasons).[72]

Fourth, to prevent any outbreak of major new conflict within or between states in the region, with all the suffering that this would involve for the peoples concerned, and all the disruptive effects this would have on the world economy and on international stability. This applies especially to those countries bordering on our allies in Central Europe. The United States has a vital interest in preventing any new conflict or armed tension in the former Soviet Union that will draw troops and attention away from areas that are truly vital to America. Above all, any possibility of U.S. soldiers fighting Russians in Russia's backyard (which in the worst-case scenario is what NATO membership for Ukraine, and our present relationship with Georgia, could eventually lead to) should be categorically excluded. After all, the historical precedents for this are not exactly positive: Hitler, Napoleon, and Sweden's Charles XII—in case anyone has forgotten.

Other than these, the United States has no vital interests and hence no "priorities" in dealing with Russia. All other interests are secondary and can be adjusted to accommodate Russia if that country accommodates the United States where this is genuinely important to us.[73]

Thus the only vital U.S. interest in Ukraine is not to promote a pro-American "democracy" there, and still less to turn Ukraine into a buffer against Russia. It is to prevent Ukraine from sinking into conflict. Of course, by the same token it is also a vital U.S. interest to prevent any Russian armed action within or against Ukraine—a clear red line must be drawn here—but it is America's own attempt at the expansion of its military alliance system at Russia's expense that is the sole likely cause of such a radically dangerous Russian move.

We argue therefore that while NATO membership for Ukraine should not be permanently excluded, there should be no question of membership for Ukraine or any other state of the former Soviet Union until two very difficult conditions are met. This clear diplomatic line would remove the present uncertainty in the region about NATO expansion. At present this uncertainty causes destabilization, by accentuating Russian fears, by raising other states' expectations to unrealistic heights, and by encouraging them to take a tough line against Russia even when this is neither necessary nor wise.

First, these countries must be ready at the same time to join the European Union. In order to join the European Union, the former Soviet states would have had to already transform themselves in a Western direction, including the establishment of real democracies, law-governed free markets, working civil societies, and peaceful and respectful relations with minorities. This is the only assurance that in making security guarantees to such states, a U.S. administration is not committing lives and treasure to defend not only unstable allies, but also countries that are likely to disintegrate, involving America in serious and unnecessary dangers.[74]

Secondly, NATO and EU membership must be acceptable not just to majorities in the countries concerned, but to majorities in all their chief regions and communities. For as we ought surely to have learned from the Yugoslav experience, a simple mathematical majority on a critical issue counts for nothing if a large minority hates that decision so much that they are prepared to take up arms against it. These conditions would postpone NATO membership for so long that there would be a good chance that by the time it became a reality, this would no longer be a serious problem between Russia and the West.

Certainly President Putin's change of course, toward the more authoritarian model of Chinese capitalism, is not ideal. But it is still an open question as to whether this change may not in fact help over time to establish the basis for a successful middle-class economy and a stable Russian democracy. At the very least, it can hardly do worse than the deeply corrupt, crime-ridden, unstable, oligarchical course Russia followed in the 1990s under President Yeltsin. During that period, Russia was obviously heading toward the kind of permanently rotten pseudo-democracy experienced by the Philippines and some Latin American countries—states where, not surprisingly, periods of democracy are regularly interrupted by military coups or outbursts of authoritarian nationalist populism like Hugo Chávez's movement in Venezuela.[75]

Part of the Great Capitalist Peace strategy involves freezing and managing existing difficulties with Russia while the magic of capitalism hopefully does its work over the next generation. If present rates of Russian economic growth continue, there is a good chance that they will eventually create a Russia so economically successful and integrated into the world economy that many of the issues now dividing Washington and Moscow literally won't seem worth fighting over anymore.

To bring that day forward, we recommend that in the meantime America and the leading Western European states should seek to extend to the European continent as a whole the idea of a concert of power, with Russia included (whereas at present Russia is excluded from both the European Union and NATO). To this end, we should seriously examine the idea of creating a European Security Council, with the United States, Russia, Turkey, Britain, France, and Germany as members, and the European Union, NATO, the Organization for Security and Cooperation in Europe (OSCE), and the Commonwealth of Independent States (CIS) as observers, and with veto powers for all the participants. Such an organization would focus on Russia and the former Soviet states, as all the major players mentioned have extensive interests in the region.[76]

This would alleviate a key Russian anxiety, which is that at present they find themselves automatically outvoted in every European forum, in a way that certainly does not reflect their actual and historical power and influence. This anxiety is a feeling with which the United States should have some sympathy, since it precisely mirrors American anger at being repeatedly, reflexively outvoted in the United Nations and various Latin American bodies.

However, the creation of such a body would not only be conciliatory to Russia, it would also provide a means of providing Turkey with a role commensurate with its own history and power, and softening what may well be an indefinite Turkish wait for EU membership. And such a European Security Council would not be just a way of soothing hurt Turkish and Russian pride. It would also be a more effective means of conducting serious, adult negotiations to solve festering conflicts like Kosovo, Abkhazia, and Nagorno-Karabakh. More effective, anyway, than the present unreal and hypocritical legalisms too often espoused by the West.[77]

This assessment should not be seen as an apology for Russian behavior where this is genuinely out of line with standard international practice. The United States should continue to both publicly and privately urge Russia, for example, to curb its excesses in Chechnya.[78] But it does mean that closer cooperation with Russia over nonproliferation and nuclear security should take precedence over dangerous fantasies and megalomaniac ambitions like quickly including Ukraine and Georgia in NATO years or decades before these countries are ready, or establishing an exclusive U.S. sphere of influence in Central Asia. If the Great Capitalist Peace is to be realized, then at its core must be cooperation with Russia for the sake of combating extremism and maintaining peace in the former Soviet Union.

China

With annual growth rates regularly exceeding 9 percent of GDP, the largest military force in the world, and now the third highest defense spending, Beijing rightly describes itself as a rising power. In other words, while the Chinese know that they are not yet the match of the United States, even in East Asia, they believe that time is on their side. Their goal is not to anger the Americans too much in the medium term, while growing relatively stronger year by year.[79]

Meanwhile, China's $800 billion in currency reserves and growing share of the U.S. public debt give Beijing a potent weapon with which to strike the U.S. economy if relations deteriorate. American moves to isolate China economically would do terrible damage to China, and could well bring down the Communist system there— but they would also bring the American economy down in ruins.

Heeding Eisenhower's warnings about fiscal security being as important as military security, America should take steps to reduce both its budget deficit and its trade deficit with China. Its approach to the latter, however, should be gradual and incremental, so as to strengthen America's position without triggering a disastrous trade war. From this point of view, it is also important to note that while in recent times the United States has focused on China's growing strength, China's enduring weaknesses could also cause serious problems for America. Many Americans would welcome the collapse of the Communist regime in Beijing. They might welcome it a bit less if they understood what the resulting economic crisis would be likely to do to American living standards and the value of the dollar.

Of all the relationships with great powers America has to manage, the Sino-American relationship may therefore be the most fraught with peril in the long term. It is this relationship, more than any other, that will determine the ultimate success or failure of the Great Capitalist Peace. If the bad news is that the clock may be ticking toward confrontation, the good news is that the United States has some genuine inducements to offer that may convince Beijing to stick to its present strategy of developing as a status quo power, rather than a revolutionary power seeking to overthrow the existing order and replace it with Chinese regional or even global hegemony.[80]

The key to maintaining a stable and peaceful Sino-American relationship, and through this to guaranteeing peace and stability in East Asia, is a recognition by both Washington and Beijing of three essential truths. Americans must recognize that domination of East Asia is now impossible. China is already simply too strong. For example, for four years now, China, not the United States, has been the chief trading partner of both South Korea and Japan. Already in 1997, China played a key part in shoring up financial stability in East and Southeast Asia during the economic crisis there. The Chinese must recognize, however, that it is equally impossible for them to replace American domination with their own unilateral hegemony. Even if America did not have an important stake and presence in the region, Japan and Vietnam have both been successfully resisting Chinese domination for more than a thousand years, and both are in their different ways regional great powers.

Finally, both Americans and Chinese must recognize that no possible gains to either from a clash between them could compensate for the damage that such a clash would do to both their economies. Indeed, the damage would probably be such as to wreck America's capacity for global leadership, and end for decades China's hopes of emerging as a great economic power on the world stage.[81]

But if there is no doubt that China is rising, that is where agreement over Sino-American relations ends in Washington. The fundamental and controversial questions are: Should the United States oppose China's rise or accommodate it and seek to shape it? And should the United States deal with a rising Beijing through carrots or sticks?[82]

The first question is easy for ethical realists—China will emerge as a great power whether the United States opposes it or not; domestic grandstanding leading to a futile policy of trying to stop the unstoppable amounts to a moral abdication of leadership. The issue therefore should not be whether China can be stopped from emerging as a great power—that has already been decided. Rather the question is whether it will be a status quo power, part of the Great Capitalist Peace, or emerge as a revolutionary power intent on challenging American power in East Asia and beyond.

While neoconservatives and their liberal hawk allies alternate between strategies of democracy promotion, containment, and confrontation, pragmatists stress the economic carrot of free trade inducements to co-opt Beijing into the American-led world order. The ethical realist answer is to use various means to change the calculations of the Chinese leadership over time. Only such an integrated strategy is likely to forestall a longer-term revolutionary Chinese challenge to the present order in East Asia and even the world.

"Balance and integrate" has been the basic strategy pursued by Washington toward Beijing over the past generation, under both Democratic and Republican administrations. Deputy Secretary of State Robert Zoellick reformulated this in 2005 as a strategy of urging China to become a "responsible stakeholder" in the international system.

Basically, this is a very good approach. China's rise just means that the strategy needs to be recalibrated, and focused more on

particular regional and economic issues. Given the risks of unnecessary and unintended clashes between them—like the EP-3 recon-
naissance plane crisis of 2001—Washington and Beijing also need
to explore all possible avenues for mutual confidence-building and
reassurance.

For this strategy to work, however, the U.S. establishment—and
even Zoellick himself—also needs to learn a new language toward
Beijing, one that patronizes and lectures a good deal less. As China's
strength grows, this is one thing the Chinese will not tolerate,
and it could do serious and unnecessary harm to the relationship.
Washington should press the Chinese government concerning product and intellectual piracy issues, and other instances where China
is clearly not playing by the international trading rules. However,
lecturing the Chinese about how to run their economy, or blaming
them, rather than America's spendthrift ways, for the current
account deficit is wrongheaded and counterproductive.[83]

On the military front, given the freedom of maneuver resulting from its present military preeminence, the United States ought
to increase security cooperation with more East and Southeast
Asian states. These relationships must, however, be clearly stated
to be defensive and involve only bilateral ties, and not an anti-
Chinese alliance on the NATO model. This would make it clear to
China that an attack on Taiwan would have severe repercussions
for China's influence and interests in the region, but without suggesting that the United States intends to create an anti-Chinese
alliance irrespective of actual Chinese behavior.

Any effort to formalize a regional multilateral alliance against
Beijing would permanently alienate China, while also forcing the
countries of the region to choose sides openly and permanently—
something they are desperately anxious not to do, even while they
do want discreetly to hedge against China's growing power.[84] A
radical and open alliance strategy is therefore bound to hurt Washington more than Beijing, and is also impractical given the divisions in the pro-American camp caused by Japan's stubborn refusal

to face up to its atrocious war record, which still unsettles such would-be allies as South Korea.

In particular, the United States should bolster its relationship with India, the other rising power in Asia. The new Indian link is especially important, as over time close U.S.-Indian ties could help deter even a bellicose Chinese leadership. By loosely acting in concert with such a regional grouping of powers, America will greatly raise the likely costs of any future Chinese adventurism, and encourage China to increase its influence incrementally within the bounds of the existing East Asian order, rather than seeking to overturn that order by force. At present, this is indeed the strategy being pursued by Beijing, through its own multilateral initiatives such as the East Asia Summit and the Shanghai Cooperation Organization.[85]

The Chinese official rubric for its current strategy is "China's Peaceful Rise." As long as they genuinely stick with that strategy, we should not move explicitly to build alliances against them. To do so would only strengthen the hands of hard-liners in the Chinese military and party establishments who reject the "Peaceful Rise" strategy and want a much tougher and more militarized approach to solving the Taiwan issue and competition with the United States.[86]

Other significant changes in American regional strategy are also necessary. With a South Korea in which most of the people amazingly no longer view Pyongyang as a threat, and with resentment of the U.S. troops based there at an all-time high, the United States should begin to significantly draw down its troop levels on the Korean peninsula. This will remove the possibility that China could ever again attack U.S. forces in a ground war, and allow the United States to concentrate instead on maintaining its present overwhelming lead over China in naval and air power.[87]

The nineteenth-century British example is instructive—just as Britain never dreamed of fighting a ground war on its own against great land powers, so the United States is also a maritime power, and should refrain at almost all costs from risking land war with Russia or China (or even Iran). Given that North Korea is increasingly China's (and South Korea's) problem, the only point in having U.S. troops on the Korean peninsula is to serve as a trip wire to stop North Korean adventurism, not to retain a puny toehold on the Asian mainland to let the Chinese know who remains boss. America should draw down troops in South Korea, and eventually withdraw them altogether, as they no longer serve a constructive purpose, while they provide China with an obvious target in the event of hostilities over Taiwan.[88]

We must be clear, however, that this withdrawal would also mean ceding to China the dominant role both in containing North Korea's nuclear ambitions and in managing the eventual collapse of the North Korean state and the appallingly difficult and expensive process of the reunification of the two Koreas. Given just how costly and difficult that has proved for the much richer Germans after the fall of the Berlin Wall, we should in fact be only too happy to throw this particular time bomb into China's lap. It would grant them international prestige and an extra share of regional influence in an area vital to their interests, while saving us great costs and dangers. North Korea therefore must be treated as a regional problem to be managed by a regional concert of powers, with China in the lead.

Further, if China is to acquiesce in the Great Capitalist Peace, America must move beyond the present Washington consensus of—practically if not formally—supporting a two-China policy over Taiwan. Here we must also be clear. In his magnificent career, the only major mistake Secretary of State Dean Acheson made was to be vague about whether South Korea lay within America's security perimeter. His confused answer encouraged the North Korean invasion of the South.

That is very much not what we are saying here. The defense of Taiwan from Chinese invasion, a fifty-five-year-old commitment, should remain entirely in force. Quite apart from the shattering blow to American pride and prestige if China were to get away with an invasion, we have given the people of Taiwan our word, and we should keep it. Taipei assuredly does lie within the American security perimeter. However, America needs to combine this ironclad commitment with much stronger moves to reduce tension with China over the island, and to discourage Taiwan from moving toward formal independence.[89] And all future administrations need to enforce discipline on their members over this. In the past, clashing American official voices have encouraged Beijing to suspect that the government in Washington has been pursuing inconsistent policies, or even practicing outright deceit.[90]

American administrations should therefore declare publicly and repeatedly that the United States does not just recognize one China legally and in theory, but actively believes that China should be reunited. They should commit America to support the reunification of the two Chinas, as long as this takes place in a peaceful and agreed manner. The line to China on this should stress that in the context of China's long history, even a few generations of Taiwanese independence are only a temporary interlude. This approach should play on Beijing's current penchant for patient, long games.

The Chinese administration should be reassured that America is not seeking to freeze the existing status quo in Taiwan's favor. They should, however, also be reminded that given the fact that Taiwan is protected by the sea, and China's naval forces for a long time to come will remain relatively weak, even a China-Taiwan war in which the United States did not come to Taiwan's aid would be a chancy and bloody affair. It would also, of course, have a shatteringly disruptive effect on the East Asian and global economies. An attack on Taiwan would therefore be contrary to China's responsibilities as a great power and aspirations to have Beijing's leadership recognized by other Asian nations.

Washington must therefore actively discourage the independence of Taiwan, as that disastrous move, in the face of Taipei's evershrinking defense budget, could only be underwritten by American sacrifice. Taiwan has every right to do whatever its leadership and people decide on the question of independence, but they must then live with the consequences. They must be made certain that America would never underwrite such a destabilization of East Asia and the global economy.

This move would reassure the Chinese leadership, while at the same time being seen as all things by all people. Beijing will believe it will eventually annex Taipei, while given present economic, social, and cultural changes on the mainland, we believe it is possible that Taiwan can, over time, in effect reannex China, through the increase in pluralism that is already accompanying China's economic liberalization.

In the economic field, America should draw China ever further into the global financial system, while seeing to it that Beijing adheres to all the World Trade Organization rules for market openness. As China, in order to attain the full free trade benefits that WTO membership promises, is forced to follow the WTO fine print and continue to open its economy—and therefore its society too—it will most probably experience the continued growth of its middle class, as increased prosperity becomes part of the Chinese experience.

An emerging middle class is likely to make the Chinese more pluralist politically, while further exposure to the world will make Communist Party control of the country ever more problematic.[91] Neoconservatives and their liberal hawk allies rightly point to China's continued persecution of some Christians, the Falun Gong, and political dissidents. However, viewed in terms of historical progress, look how far the Chinese government, under the impetus of economic liberalization, has moved since the murderous excesses of Mao Tse-tung.

By ending the totalitarian excesses of Maoism and adopting capitalist economic reforms, Deng Xiaoping was able to propel more people into the middle class more quickly than any leader in history. Chinese society has become far more pluralistic than it was just a few decades ago, a blink of an eye in Chinese historical terms. While China is not yet democratic, surely this more subtle process of economic subversion stands a better chance of allowing China to remake itself than any pressure of ours from the outside.

Arguing with the hard-line U.S. "confrontation" school, Robert Zoellick put matters very well in 2005. While harshly criticizing China for some of its economic and security policies, he also declared,

> For fifty years our policy was to fence in the Soviet Union while its own internal contradictions undermined it. For thirty years, our policy has been to draw out the People's Republic of China. As a result, the China of today is simply not the Soviet Union of the late 1940s: It does not seek to spread radical, anti-American ideologies. While not yet democratic, it does not see itself in a twilight conflict against democracy around the world. While at times mercantilist, it does not see itself in a death struggle with capitalism. And most importantly, China does not believe that its future depends on overturning the fundamental order of the international system. In fact, quite the reverse: China's leaders have decided that their success depends on being networked with the modern world.
>
> If the Cold War analogy does not apply, neither does the distant balance-of-power politics of 19th Century Europe. The global economy of the 21st Century is a tightly woven fabric. We are too interconnected to try to hold China at arm's length, hoping to promote other powers in Asia at its expense. Nor would the other powers in fact hold China at bay, initiating and terminating ties based on an old model of drawing room diplomacy. The United States seeks constructive relations with all countries that do not threaten peace and security.[92]

This is an admirable summary of the philosophy underlying the Great Capitalist Peace, and a welcome sign that intelligent, sensible, courageous, and well-informed senior public servants still exist in America. The problem is that on every issue that we have discussed, figures like Robert Zoellick have to fight hard to save their policies from being overwhelmed by chauvinist and self-defeating approaches—and alas, they often lose. In June 2006, Zoellick announced that he was to leave the administration.

CONCLUSIONS

If we should perish, the ruthlessness of the foe would
be only the secondary cause of the disaster. The primary cause would be that the strength of a giant nation
was directed by eyes too blind to see all the hazards of
the struggle; and the blindness would be induced not by
some accident of nature or history, but by hatred and
vainglory.

—REINHOLD NIEBUHR

In this book, we have argued that in certain respects the situation
facing America today resembles that at the beginning of the Cold
War, and demands a similarly revolutionary shift in structures
and priorities. We have had high praise for Truman, Eisenhower,
and some of their key lieutenants. But even under such leadership,
the record of these administrations was not perfect. George Kennan himself, like Niebuhr, Morgenthau, and many of the intellectual supporters of containment, came to deeply regret that such
primacy had been given to the military aspects of the struggle, and
that rigidity and paranoia had come to characterize so much of U.S.
policy.

There were individual mistakes, like Acheson's failure to explicitly include South Korea in America's security perimeter in Asia,
and there were grave lapses of moral judgment, like the Eisenhower administration's overthrow of elected governments in Iran
and Guatemala. The consequences of these were very bad for U.S.

interests and honor, and absolutely disastrous for the countries concerned.

Today, with the American homeland threatened by catastrophic terrorism, the world economy dancing merrily along a tightrope over a chasm, and China rising as a potential competitor with the United States, the stakes are, if anything, even higher than they were in the late 1940s and early 1950s, and our room for error is less. Yet since 9/11 the quality of the response by the administration and the leading groups of both main parties has been pitiful by comparison with that of their illustrious predecessors.

When it comes to the existing and dangerous state of relations between major countries in the world today, we are also haunted by another image: that of the outbreak of the First World War in 1914, when a generation of young Europeans destroyed one another, wrecked several of their countries, and came close to destroying European civilization.

Looking back at the statesmen who led their respective countries into this catastrophe, the obvious question must surely be, "How can they have been so stupid?" No truly vital national interest of any of the countries involved justified the horrible risks of general war. In retrospect, the very thought of great civilized empires going to war for the sake of control over the Balkans, the flashpoint of the conflict, creates a kind of sick bemusement. And indeed, in the course of the conflict several formerly "vital" interests turned out not to be vital after all. Thus Britain was prepared to surrender Constantinople to Russia, although in the past sixty years it had three times waged or threatened war with Russia to prevent just this.

Equally important, unlike the Second World War (or our struggle with Islamist extremism of the Al Qaeda stamp), the First World War was not a battle for civilization on either side. The ruling classes of all the major European states of the time were basically similar in their culture. They were warlike by contemporary standards, but also civilized and restrained. As a result of the war they launched, their culture was crippled, and replaced in several countries by ideologies and tyrants so monstrous that the British

Edwardians and their continental equivalents could scarcely have imagined them in their worst nightmares.

If that is indeed an excuse for the folly of the generation of 1914, then it is an excuse that we in 2006 lack. Unlike them, we are not living at the end of a long century of Western middle-class peace, comfort, and progress. After the experiences of the past one hundred years, we know perfectly well what a thin line sometimes separates civilization and utter barbarism, even in the West. After 9/11, we know the extent of the terrorist threat to civilization in general. We have had some strong warnings of the capacity of terrorism to undermine and even destroy our democracies by provoking paranoia and authoritarianism.

Successfully prosecuting the war on terror and establishing a largely peaceful global order will require the great powers of the world to stop playing stupid and irrelevant geopolitical games against one another—and it is for the United States, as the greatest of the great powers, to take the lead. Contemporary U.S. power gives America a level of responsibility for the future of the planet that should automatically involve a sense of prudence, of stewardship, and of the need for consultation with the rest of mankind.

As Truman and Eisenhower both knew, the questions surrounding America's global role are profoundly moral ones, and not matters for political posturing and domestic grandstanding. If with all its power and wealth, the American establishment of today fails in its duty to preserve the Great Capitalist Peace for future generations, then those generations won't waste their sympathy on our need to advance our careers and please our constituents and financial backers. They will simply consign us to the ash heap along with the other worthless powers of history.

This would be a tragedy, not just for America, but for the world, for America and its democratic example are indeed in many ways, as Lincoln said, "The last, best hope of mankind." Ethical realism and the Great Capitalist Peace are not just strategies for staving off American decline. They form a blueprint for America to live up to its glorious national promise.

Notes

Introduction

1. Hillary Rodham Clinton, "Challenges for U.S. Foreign Policy in the Middle East," remarks given at Princeton University's Woodrow Wilson School of Public and International Affairs, January 19, 2006; see also Senator Evan Bayh, speech at the Center for Strategic and International Studies, Washington, D.C., February 2, 2006.
2. Reinhold Niebuhr, *The Irony of American History* (New York: Charles Scribner and Sons, 1952), p. 42.
3. Francis Fukuyama, *America at the Crossroads: Democracy, Power, and the Neoconservative Legacy* (New Haven: Yale University Press, 2006).
4. Edmund Burke, "Remarks on the Policy of the Allies with Respect to France," in *The Works of the Right Honourable Edmund Burke*, vol. 4, at www.gutenberg.org/files/15700/15700-0.txt.
5. Reinhold Niebuhr, *Christian Realism and Political Problems* (1953; repr.: Fairfield, N.J.: Augustus M. Kelley, 1977), p. 106.

Chapter 1: Lessons of the Truman-Eisenhower Moment

1. Quoted in Walter Isaacson and Evan Thomas, *The Wise Men: Six Friends and the World They Made* (New York: Simon & Schuster, 1986), p. 519.
2. Quotations from Kennan's essay in this chapter are from "The Sources of Soviet Conduct," by X, *Foreign Affairs*, July 1947.
3. For the background to the telegram, see Hugh Thomas, *Armed Truce: The Beginnings of the Cold War, 1945–46* (New York: Sceptre, 1986), pp. 675–78.
4. For Truman's speech to Congress setting out the basis of the doctrine (in connection with aid to Greece and Turkey) on March 12, 1947, see cnn.com/SPECIALS/cold.war/episodes/03/documents/Truman/.
5. See Thomas, *Armed Truce*, pp. 285–327, 693–711.

6. David McCullough, *Truman* (New York: Simon & Schuster, 1992), p. 980.

7. Isaacson and Thomas, *The Wise Men*, p. 29.

8. Thomas, *Armed Truce*, p. 300.

9. Quoted in Isaacson and Thomas, *The Wise Men*, pp. 412–13.

10. Quoted in Gilbert, *Churchill: A Life* (New York: Owl Books, 1992), p. 894.

11. Quoted in McCullough, *Truman*, p. 583.

12. Quoted in ibid., p. 564.

13. Quoted in Isaacson and Thomas, *The Wise Men*, pp. 432–33.

14. Quoted in McCullough, *Truman*, p. 514.

15. Quoted in Isaacson and Thomas, *The Wise Men*, p. 374.

16. Quoted in McCullough, *Truman*, p. 665.

17. McCullough, *Truman*, p. 646.

18. Quoted in ibid., p. 775.

19. Quoted in Isaacson and Thomas, *The Wise Men*, p. 522.

20. McCullough, *Truman*, p. 847.

21. Ibid., p. 845.

22. Quoted in Isaacson and Thomas, *The Wise Men*, p. 523.

23. McCullough, *Truman*, p. 853.

24. Quoted in Isaacson and Thomas, *The Wise Men*, p. 559.

25. Quoted in Stephen E. Ambrose, *Eisenhower: Soldier and President* (New York: Simon & Schuster, 1990), p. 275.

26. Ambrose, *Eisenhower*, p. 331.

27. Quoted in Marc Trachtenberg, "A 'Wasting Asset': American Strategy and the Shifting Nuclear Balance, 1949–54," *International Security* 13, no. 3 (Winter 1988–89).

28. For an account of the project by Kennan and other participants, see William B. Pickett, ed., *George F. Kennan and the Origins of Eisenhower's New Look: An Oral History of Project Solarium* (Princeton Institute for International and Regional Studies, Monograph No. 1).

29. George F. Kennan, *Memoirs: 1950–1963* (New York: Pantheon, 1983), p. 186. See also Pickett, *George F. Kennan*. Eisenhower's questions are quoted in Trachtenberg, "A 'Wasting Asset,' " p. 40; see also Ambrose, *Eisenhower*, p. 369.

30. See Robert R. Bowie and Richard H. Immerman, *Waging Peace: How Eisenhower Shaped an Enduring Cold War Strategy* (New York: Oxford University Press, 1998), especially pp. 123–46; Ronald R. Krebs, *Dueling Visions: U.S. Strategy Toward Eastern Europe Under Eisenhower* (College Station: Texas A&M University Press, 2001).

    For the official summary of the Solarium Exercise's proceedings, see *Foreign Relations of the United States, 1952–1954*, Vol. 2,

Part 1, pp. 323–67 (Washington, D.C.: U.S. Government Printing Office, 1984).

    For the debates on military spending and the budget deficit, see especially Glenn R. Snyder, "The 'New Look' of 1953," in *Strategy, Politics and Defense Budgets,* ed. Warner R. Schilling, Paul Y. Hammond, and Glenn R. Snyder (New York: Columbia University Press, 1962).

31. Speech at Churchill's funeral.

32. Quoted in Ambrose, *Eisenhower,* p. 479.

33. Bowie and Immerman, *Waging Peace,* p. 142.

34. Quoted in Ambrose, *Eisenhower,* pp. 325–26.

35. Quoted in ibid., p. 360.

36. Quoted in ibid., p. 380.

37. Quoted in ibid.

38. McCullough, *Truman,* p. 919.

39. For parallels between the Cold War and the war on terror, see Anatol Lieven, "Lessons of the Cold War for the War on Terror," Carnegie Endowment for International Peace Policy Brief No. 7, October 2001, at carnegieendowment.org.

40. *The Final Report on the 9/11 Commission Recommendations* is to be found at www.9-11pdp.org/press/2005-12-05_report.pdf. The original 9/11 Commission report, issued in July 2004, is published by W. W. Norton.

41. See Paul Pillar, "Intelligence, Policy and the War in Iraq," *Foreign Affairs,* March–April 2006. Pillar, a career CIA officer, was national intelligence officer for the Near East and South Asia from 2000 to 2005.

42. See *Americans on Iraq: Three Years On,* poll by the Program on International Policy Issues and Knowledge Networks, March 15, 2006, at WorldPublicOpinion.org.

Chapter 2: The Failure of Rollback and Preventive War

1. Daniel Kelly, *James Burnham and the Struggle for the World: A Life* (Wilmington: ISI, 2002), p. 129. For a more sympathetic portrayal of Burnham's thought, see Samuel Francis, *Thinkers of Our Time: James Burnham* (London: Claridge, 1999).

2. James Burnham, *Containment or Liberation? An Inquiry into the Aims of U.S. Foreign Policy* (New York: John Day, 1952), pp. 251–54.

3. Kelly, *James Burnham,* p. 129.

4. Norman Podhoretz, *The Present Danger: Do We Have the Will to Reverse the Decline of American Power?* (New York: Simon & Schuster, 1980).

5. James Burnham, *The Struggle for the World* (New York: John Day, 1947), p. 148.

6. Charles Krauthammer, "The Bush Doctrine," *Time*, March 5, 2001.

7. Burnham, *The Struggle for the World*, pp. 1, 164ff.

8. Ibid, pp. 194–96; Kelly, *James Burnham*, pp. 168–70.

9. George F. Kennan, *American Diplomacy* (Chicago: University of Chicago Press, 1979), p. 164.

10. See, for example, the National Intelligence Estimate of August 9, 1960, on Sino-Soviet relations, which presents the evidence of a deep and growing split but then concludes, strangely, that this won't amount to anything really serious in the years to come. The estimate is to be found in *Tracking the Dragon: National Intelligence Estimates on China During the Era of Mao, 1948–1976*, published by the National Intelligence Council, Washington, D.C., pp. 215–48.

11. In the *Chicago Sun-Times*, November 11, 1948, quoted in Alonzo L. Hamby, *Beyond the New Deal: Harry S. Truman and American Liberalism* (New York: Columbia University Press, 1973), p. 367. For similar views by other members of the ADA, see John K. Fairbank, "China: Three Lessons," *ADA World*, September 22, 1949; ADA board statement on Asia, *ADA World*, October 1950; David C. Williams, "Chinese Fanaticism Like Yugoslavs Prior to Break with Stalin," *ADA World*, November 1950.

12. David Halberstam, *The Best and the Brightest* (New York: Ballantine, 1992), p. 339.

13. Norman Podhoretz, "World War IV: How It Started, What It Means, and Why We Have to Win," *Commentary*, September 2004.

14. Paul Berman, *Terror and Liberalism* (New York: W. W. Norton, 2003).

15. Paul Berman, *Power and the Idealists; or, The Passion of Joschka Fischer and Its Aftermath* (Brooklyn, N.Y.: Soft Skull Press, 2005), quoted in Stephen Holmes, "The War of the Liberals," *Nation*, November 14, 2005.

16. For the foundation of the ADA, see Gillon, *Politics and Vision*, pp. 16–24; Mark L. Kleinman, *A World of Hope, A World of Fear: Henry A. Wallace, Reinhold Niebuhr and American Liberalism* (Columbus: Ohio State University Press, 1994), pp. 227–32; Kevin Mattson, *When America Was Great: The Fighting Faith of Postwar Liberalism* (New York: Routledge, 2004), pp. 45–46; Hamby, *Beyond the New Deal*, pp. 161–64.

17. Arthur Schlesinger Jr., *The Vital Center: The Politics of Freedom* (first published 1949; repr.: Piscataway, N.J.: Transaction Publishers, 1997).

18. Peter Beinart, "A Fighting Faith: An Argument for a New Liberalism," *New Republic*, December 13, 2004; Peter Beinart, *The Good Fight: How Liberals—And Only Liberals—Can Win the War on Terror and Make America Great Again* (New York: HarperCollins, 2006).

19. Peter Beinart, "Tough Liberalism," *Blueprint*, Progressive Policy Institute, October 21, 2005.

20. See Ari Berman, "The Strategic Class," *Nation*, August 29, 2005.

21. See Anatol Lieven, "We Do Not Deserve These People," *London Review of Books*, October 20, 2005.

22. See Sam Rosenfeld and Matthew Iglesias, "The Incompetence Dodge," *American Prospect*, November 10, 2005.

23. Beinart, *The Good Fight*, p. 286.

24. See Anatol Lieven and David Chambers, "The Limits of Propaganda," *Los Angeles Times*, February 13, 2006; Neil MacFarquhar, "Washington's Arabic TV Effort Gets Mixed Reviews," *New York Times*, February 19, 2004; Faye Bowers, "Al Hurra Joins Battle for Hearts and Minds," *Christian Science Monitor*, February 24, 2004; "US Voice in Arabia: Washington's Arabic Satellite TV Station Has Run into Trouble," *Financial Times*, November 9, 2005; Anne Marie Baylouny, "Alhurra, the Free One: Assessing U.S. Satellite Television in the Middle East," *Strategic Insights* 4, no. 11 (November 2005).

25. For the "non-Communist left" strategy, see Schlesinger, *The Vital Center*, pp. 143–56.

Chapter 3: Ethical Realism

1. Reinhold Niebuhr, *The Irony of American History* (New York: Scribner, 1985), p. 160.

2. Hans J. Morgenthau, *Politics Among Nations* (New York: McGraw-Hill, 2005), p. 10.

3. For overviews of ethical realist thought, see Joel H. Rosenthal and Kenneth W. Thompson, *Righteous Realists: Political Realism, Responsible Power, and American Culture in the Nuclear Age* (Baton Rouge: Louisiana State University Press, 1991); and Robin Lovin, *Reinhold Niebuhr and Christian Realism* (New York: Cambridge University Press, 1995).

4. Niebuhr, *The Irony of American History*, p. 5.

5. Reinhold Niebuhr, "Christianity and Communism: Social Justice," *Spectator* 157 (November 6, 1936). See also Kenneth W. Thompson, "Beyond National Interest: A Critical Evaluation of Reinhold Niebuhr's Theory of International Politics," *Review of Politics* 17 (April 1955); and Mark L. Haas, "Reinhold Niebuhr's 'Christian Pragmatism': A Principled Alternative to Consequentialism," *Review of Politics* 61, no. 4 (Autumn 1999).

6. Reinhold Niebuhr, *The Structure of Nations and Empires: A Study of Recurring Patterns and Problems of the Political Order in Relation to*

the Unique Problems of the Nuclear Age (New York: Scribner, 1959), p. 193.

7. George F. Kennan, reply to Quaker document "Speak Truth to Power," in *Progressive*, October 1955.

8. Hans J. Morgenthau, *Scientific Man and Power Politics* (Chicago: University of Chicago Press, 1967), pp. 202–3.

9. Hans J. Morganthau, "The Political Science of E. H. Carr," *World Politics* 1 (1948) quoted in A. J. H. Murray, "The Moral Politics of Hans Morganthau," *The Review of Politics* 51, no. 1 (Winter 1960). For Morgenthau's relationship to Machiavelli, see also Greg Russell, *Hans J. Morgenthau and the Ethics of American Statecraft* (Baton Rouge: Louisiana State University Press, 1990), especially pp. 148–55.

10. See Hans J. Morgenthau, "The Mind of Abraham Lincoln," in *Essays on Lincoln's Faith and Politics*, ed. Kenneth W. Thompson (Lanham, Md.: University Press of America, 1983).

11. Niebuhr, *The Irony of American History*, p. 148.

12. Robert C. Good, "The National Interest and Political Realism: Niebuhr's 'Debate' with Morgenthau and Kennan," *Journal of Politics* 22, no. 4 (November 1960); for Morgenthau's morality, see also Robert Jervis, "Hans Morgenthau, Realism, and the Scientific Study of International Politics," *Social Research* 61, no. 4 (Winter 1994).

13. Edmund Burke, *Reflections on the Revolution in France* (London: Penguin, 1979), p. 89.

14. Hans J. Morgenthau, *In Defense of the National Interest* (Lanham, Md.: University Press of America, 1982), p. 34.

15. Kennan, *American Diplomacy*, p. 177.

16. Hans J. Morgenthau, *The Purpose of American Politics* (Lanham, Md.: University Press of America), p. 42.

17. Quoted in Campbell Craig, "The New Meaning of Modern War in the Thought of Reinhold Niebuhr," *Journal of the History of Ideas* 53, no. 4 (1992).

18. Edmund Burke, *Thoughts on the Cause of the Present Discontents: Select Works of Edmund Burke.* A New Imprint of the Payne Edition. Foreword and Biographical Note by Francis Canavan, 4 vols. (Indianapolis, Ind.: Liberty Fund, 1999), p. 105.

19. Hans J. Morgenthau, *Politics Among Nations: The Struggle for Power and Peace*, 5th ed. (New York: Alfred A. Knopf, 1978), p. 12

20. Owen Harries, "Power and Morals," *Prospect* magazine (United Kingdom), April 2005.

21. For the absolute failure of the Bush administration and the Pentagon to prepare for even the most obvious scenarios in the wake of Saddam's overthrow, see, for example, George Packer, *The Assassins' Gate: America*

in Iraq (New York: Farrar, Straus & Giroux, 2005), especially pp. 100–148. For the intelligence community's warnings, see Paul Pillar, "Intelligence, Policy and the War in Iraq," *Foreign Affairs,* March–April 2006.

22. Jonathan Clarke, "The Guns of 17th Street," *National Interest,* Spring 2001.

23. Kennan, "Overdue Changes in Our Foreign Policy," *Harper's Magazine,* August 1956.

24. Charles Krauthammer, "Democratic Realism: An American Foreign Policy for a Unipolar World" (speech, American Enterprise Institute, Washington, D.C., February 12, 2004).

25. "U.S. Policy Toward Russia: Report of an Independent Task Force," March 6 2006, at cfr.org.

26. Charles Krauthammer, "To Hell with Sympathy," *Time,* November 17, 2003.

27. Reinhold Niebuhr, *The Nature and Destiny of Man,* vol. 2, Human Destiny (Louisville, Ky.: John Knox Press, 1996), p. 243.

28. J. William Fulbright, *The Arrogance of Power* (New York: Random House, 1967), p. 22.

29. Hans Morgenthau, "The Limits of Historical Justice," in *Truth and Power: Collected Essays, 1960–1970* (New York: Praeger, 1970).

30. See Peter Galbraith, "The Mess," *New York Review of Books,* 53, no. 4 (March 9, 2006).

31. See Dimitri Simes, "Jihad, Unintended," *National Interest,* Winter 2005–06.

32. Bruce Cumings, "The Origin and Political Development of the Northeast Asian Political Economy," *International Organization* 38, no. 1 (Winter 1984).

33. Kennan, *American Diplomacy,* p. 47.

34. Irving Kristol, *Reflections of a Neo-conservative* (New York: Basic Books, 1983), p. xiii.

35. Charles Maurras, *Mes Idées Politiques* (1937; repr., Paris: L'Age de l'Homme, 2002).

36. For an earlier version of this argument, see Anatol Lieven, *America Right or Wrong: An Anatomy of American Nationalism* (New York: Oxford University Press, 2004), passim.

37. Kennan, *American Diplomacy,* pp. 100–101. See also C. Vann Woodward, *The Burden of Southern History* (Baton Rouge: Louisiana State University Press, 1968), pp. 205–7.

38. Quoted in Halberstam, *The Best and the Brightest,* p. 69.

Chapter 4: The Great Capitalist Peace

1. Speech by Manmohan Singh in acceptance of an honorary doctorate at Oxford University, July 8, 2005, as reported in *The Hindu* (Delhi).

2. Michael Lind, *The American Way of Strategy: U.S. Foreign Policy and the American Way of Life* (New York: Oxford University Press, 2006).

3. George Washington, "Farewell Address to the American People," at www.yale.edu/lawweb/avalon/washing/htm.

4. Dwight D. Eisenhower, "Farewell Radio and Television Address to the American People, January 17, 1961," *Public Papers of the Presidents of the United States: Dwight D. Eisenhower, January 1, 1960–January 21, 1961* (Washington, D.C.: U.S. Government Printing Office, 1961), pp. 1035–40.

5. Niall Ferguson, *Empire: The Rise and Demise of the British World Order and Its Lessons for Global Power* (New York: Basic Books, 2004); Max Boot, *The Savage Wars of Peace: Small Wars and the Rise of American Power* (New York: Basic Books, 2003).

6. Zbigniew Brzezinski, *The Grand Chess Board: American Primacy and Its Geostrategic Imperatives* (New York: Basic Books, 1997), p. 21

7. John C. Hulsman, David Polansky, and Rachel Prager "The Rebirth of Realism and the Lessons of History: The British Example," *The National Interest*, Fall 2003.

8. For the text of the Anglo-Russian agreement, see Great Britain, *Parliamentary Papers*, vol. 125, Cmd. 3750 (London, 1908), in the World War I Document Archive on the server of the Brigham Young University Library.

9. Paul Kennedy, *The Rise and Fall of the Great Powers: Economic Change and Military Conflict from 1500 to 2000* (New York: HarperCollins, 1989), p. 297. See also Aaron L. Friedberg, *The Weary Titan: Britain and the Experience of Relative Decline, 1895–1905* (Princeton: Princeton University Press, 1988); and Michael Howard, *The Continental Commitment* (London: Temple South, 1972).

10. Martin Wolf, "The Failure to Calculate the True Costs of War," *Financial Times*, January 10, 2006; Wolf's article was based on the paper "The Economic Costs of the Iraq War: An Appraisal Three Years After the End of the Conflict," by Linda Bilmes and Joseph E. Stiglitz (Allied Social Science Associations, Boston, January 2006).

11. Rudyard Kipling, "Arithmetic on the Frontier," *The Complete Verse* (London: Kyle Cathie, 1996), p. 36.

12. George Kennan, quoted in Ivan Eland, *The Empire Has No Clothes: U.S. Foreign Policy Exposed* (Washington, D.C.: The Independent Institute, 2004). For Kennan's views on NATO enlargement, see also his "The New

Russia as a New Neighbor" in Kennan, *At a Century's Ending* (New York: W. W. Norton, 1996), pp. 320–33; and the exchange of letters "Marooned in the Cold War," with Mark Danner, Strobe Talbott, and Lee H. Hamilton in *World Policy Journal* 15, no. 1 (Fall 1997).

13. For the roots of this belief in the "American Creed" and the history of American civic nationalism, see Lieven, *America Right or Wrong*, pp. 48–87; Louis Hartz, *The Liberal Tradition in America* (New York: Harcourt Brace Jovanovich, 1955), pp. 225–37; Ernest Lee Tuveson, *Redeemer Nation: The Idea of America's Millennial Role* (Chicago: University of Chicago Press, 1968). See also Walter A. McDougall, *Promised Land, Crusader State: The American Encounter with the World Since 1776* (Boston: Houghton Mifflin, 1997), pp. 81ff.

14. For the history of America's democratizing mission, see Tony Smith, *America's Mission: The United States and the Worldwide Struggle for Democracy in the Twentieth Century* (Princeton: Princeton University Press, 1994).

15. For the religious nature of the imagery of the "path to democracy and the free market," see Anatol Lieven, *Chechnya: Tombstone of Russian Power* (New Haven: Yale University Press, 1998), pp. 8–11; and Harvey Cox, "The Market as God," *Atlantic Monthly*, March 1999; see also Samuel Huntington, *The Clash of Civilizations and the Remaking of the World Order* (New York: Simon & Schuster, 1996), especially pp. 19–39, 183–206, 301–22.

16. For earlier versions of this belief with regard to Iran, see Abbas Milani, Larry Diamond, and Michael McFaul, "A Blurred Vision: The US failure to Articulate a Coherent Policy Toward Iran Works Against the Goal of Democratic Change," *Los Angeles Times*, July 20, 2003; Reuel Marc Gerecht, "Going Soft on Iran: The Temptation of America's Foreign Policy 'Realists,' " *Weekly Standard*, March 8, 2004.

17. See Frank Gaffney "The Middle East and the 2004 Presidential Elections" (address, 57th Conference of the Middle East Institute, Washington, D.C., October 23, 2003, transcript at www.mideasti.org/articles). Natan Sharansky, *The Case for Democracy: The Power of Freedom to Overcome Tyranny and Terror* (New York: Public Affairs, 2004). For the impact on Bush, and especially the inaugural speech of 2005, see Peter Baker, "Bush Doctrine Is Expected to Get Chilly Reception," *Washington Post*, January 23, 2005; Anatol Lieven, "Warped Advice Blights American Intervention," *Financial Times*, March 16, 2005; Michael Novak, "A Bold and Brave Advance," *National Review* online, March 1, 2005. For the general progress of the administration's democratization strategy as of the start of 2006, see the debate "Freedom Crusade, Revisited," in *National Interest*, Winter 2005–06.

18. See Samantha M. Shapiro, "The War Within the Arab Newsroom," *New York Times*, January 2, 2005.

19. Max Boot, "Project for a New Chinese Century: Beijing Plans for National Greatness," *Weekly Standard*, October 10, 2005.

20. Elie Kedourie, *Nationalism* (London: Hutchinson, 1979), pp. 15–16; Lieven, *America Right or Wrong*, pp. 80–84; William Pfaff, *Barbarian Sentiments: America in the New Century* (New York: Farrar, Straus & Giroux, 2000), pp. 270–71.

21. See National Security Strategy (NSS) 2006, p. 3.

22. See Condoleezza Rice, "Transforming the Middle East," *Washington Post*, August 7, 2003; George Melloan, "Protecting Human Rights Is a Valid Foreign Policy Goal," *Wall Street Journal* (Global View), June 10, 2003; "A Wilsonian Call for Freedom," *Washington Times* editorial, November 7, 2003; Joshua Muravchik, "Bringing Democracy to the Arab World," *Current History*, January 2004.

23. Edward D. Mansfield and Jack Snyder, *Electing to Fight: Why Emerging Democracies Go to War* (Cambridge, Mass.: MIT Press, 2005).

24. Franklin D. Roosevelt, "Annual Message to Congress, January 6, 1941," Franklin D. Roosevelt Presidential Library and Museum, at http://www.fdrlibrary.marist.edu/4free.html.

25. John C. Calhoun, *A Disquisition on Government and Selections from the Discourse*, C. Gordon Post, ed. (Indianapolis, Ind.: Hackett, 1995), p. 41.

26. The annual "Freedom in the World" surveys are to be found at www.freedomhouse.org.

27. NSS 2006, pp. 35, 36.

28. Ron Suskind, *The Price of Loyalty: George W. Bush, the White House and the Education of Paul O'Neill* (New York: Simon & Schuster, 2004); Richard A. Clarke, *Against All Enemies: Inside America's War on Terror* (New York: Free Press, 2004); Richard A. Clarke and Rand Beers, *The Forgotten Homeland* (New York: Century Foundation, 2006); Michael Scheuer, *Imperial Hubris: Why the West Is Losing the War on Terror* (Dulles, Va.: Potomac Books, 2004); Robin Wright, "Top Focus Before 9/11 Wasn't on Terrorism," *Washington Post*, April 1, 2004.

29. Ambrose, *Eisenhower*, p. 344.

30. Sergei Lavrov, "Russia in Global Politics," *Moskovskiye Novosti*, March 3, 2006, translated by the Russian Ministry of Foreign Affairs.

31. Walter Russell Mead, "The US-EU Split," address to the New America Foundation, February 13, 2003 (New America Foundation program brief). See also Samuel Eliot Morison, *Oxford History of the American People*, Vol. 3 (New York: Penguin, 1994), p. 149. For America's overall imperial strategy since the end of the Cold War, see Andrew J. Bacevich,

American Empire: The Realities and Consequences of U.S. Diplomacy (Cambridge: Harvard University Press, 2002). For the full neoconservative version of this global program, see David Frum and Richard Perle, *An End to Evil: How to Win the War on Terror* (New York: Random House, 2003).

32. For an earlier version of this thesis, see Anatol Lieven, "The Secret Policeman's Ball: The U.S., Russia, and the International Order After September 11," *International Affairs* 78, no. 2 (Summer 2002).

33. The classic statement of this argument was by Norman Angell, in *The Great Illusion* (New York: Putnam & Sons, 1913).

34. See Dominic Lieven, *The Aristocracy in Europe, 1815–1914* (London: Macmillan, 1992), pp. 181–202.

Chapter 5: The Way Forward

1. Morgenthau, *Politics Among Nations*, p. 531.

2. For an interesting discussion of the U.S.-Russia-China triangle, see "America, China, and Russia," a roundtable discussion with Dr. Christopher Marsh at the Nixon Center, March 10, 2003, at www.nixoncenter.org.

3. Private discussion with Anatol Lieven.

4. See Barry C. Lynn, "War, Trade and Utopia," *National Interest*, Winter 2005–06.

5. See Victor Mallet, "Heed the Warnings of a New Cold War in Asia," *Financial Times*, March 28, 2006; M. K. Bhadrakumar, "Reheating the Cold War," *Asia Times*, March 24, 2006. Agence France-Presse, "Russia's Newfound Clout Pushes US to Rethink Ties," Washington, March 28, 2006; Dmitriy Furman: "A Cold War Without Words: Democratic Camouflage Keeps Russia from Properly Formulating Its Real Policy in CIS," *Nezavisimaya Gazeta*, March 27, 2006. For a critique of these new Cold War sentiments as directed against Russia, see also Anatol Lieven, "Why Are We Trying to Reheat the Cold War?," *Los Angeles Times*, March 19, 2006. For the Russian-Chinese relationship, see Mike Ekel, "Russian President Seeks Deeper Ties with China as U.S. Criticizes Both," Associated Press, March 20, 2006.

6. For a different variant of the concert idea, see Lind, *The American Way of Strategy*, pp. 261–81.

7. See Michael Ryan Kraig, "Forging a New Security Order for the Persian Gulf," *Middle East Policy* 12, no. 1 (Spring 2006).

8. For a strategy of offshore balancing, see Stephen M. Walt, *Taming American Power: The Global Response to U.S. Primacy* (New York: W. W. Norton, 2005).

9. Karim Sadjadpour, "Iran's Paradoxical Yearning for America," *Daily Star* (Beirut), December 4, 2004. See also Afshin Molavi, "Our Allies in Iran," *New York Times,* November 3, 2005.

10. Historian Bernard Lewis, advising Vice President Dick Cheney, as reported by Evan Thomas, "The Twelve Year Itch," *Newsweek,* March 31, 2003. For parallels with how the United States treated Vietnamese nationalism during the war there, see Halberstam, *The Best and the Brightest,* p. 125.

11. For a portrait of the complexity of political Islam even in Saudi Arabia, see Stephane Lacroix, "Between Islamists and Liberals: Saudi Arabia's new "Islamo-Liberal Reformists," *Middle East Journal* 58, no. 3 (Summer 2004).

12. See the regional surveys of the Pew Global Attitudes project, at pewresearch.org. The findings are summarized in Andrew Kohut, *Testimony to U.S. House International Relations Committee,* Subcommittee on Oversight and Investigations, November 10, 2005.

13. Zawahiri's letter quoted in Peter Bergen, *The Osama bin Laden I Know: An Oral History of al Qaeda's Leader* (New York: Free Press, 2006), pp. 365–67.

14. See John C. Hulsman, "Waiting for Godot: Or Why I Learned to Quit Worrying and Love the CAP," *Sprout* 2, no. 1 (September 2003).

15. Tom Ricker, "Competition or Massacre? Central American Farmers' Dismal Prospects Under CAFTA," *Multinational Monitor* 25, no. 4 (April 2004), at http://multinationalmonitor.org/mm2004/04012004/april04corp1.html.

16. See "Pakistan Asks US to Suspend Textile Barriers," *Pakistan Tribune* (Islamabad), October 2004; Robert Looney, "Problems in Using Trade to Counter Terrorism: The Case of Pakistan," *Strategic Insights* 1, no. 8 (October 2002).

17. See Beinart, *The Good Fight,* pp. 178–79, 278ff; Paul Blustein, "U.S. Free Trade Deals Include Few Muslim Countries," *Washington Post,* December 3, 2004.

18. See Robert Zoellick, "Countering Terror with Trade," *Washington Post,* September 20, 2001.

19. See "Trouble on the Waterfront," *Economist,* February 25, 2006.

20. Marc A. Miles, Edwin J. Feulner, and Mary Anastasia O'Grady, *2005 Index of Economic Freedom* (Washington, D.C.: Heritage Foundation and Wall Street Journal, 2005).

21. See Jeremy M. Sharp, "The Middle East Partnership Initiative: An Overview," Congressional Research Service Report for Congress, February 8, 2005; Tamara Cofman Wittes and Sarah E. Yerkes, "The Middle

East Partnership Initiative: Progress, Problems and Prospects," Saban Center Middle East Memo No. 5, November 29, 2004.

22. Cumings, "The Origin and Political Development" pp. 24–25; Robert Wade, *Governing the Market: Economic Theory and the Role of Government in East Asian Industrialization* (Princeton: Princeton University Press, 1990), pp. 82ff.

23. George Perkovich, "Giving Justice Its Due: The Missing Principle," *Foreign Affairs,* July–August 2005; Afshin Molavi, "Dignity, Above All," *Arab Trends,* October 21, 2004.

24. Benjamin M. Friedman, *The Moral Consequences of Economic Growth* (New York: Alfred A. Knopf, 2005), especially pp. 297–326, 346–68; Joseph E. Stiglitz, "The Ethical Economist," *Foreign Affairs,* November–December 2005.

25. Aristotle, *The Politics,* book 4, trans. William Ellis, pp. 12–13, at http://www.gutenberg.org/dirs/etext04/tgovt10.txt.

26. See Nancy Birdsall, "Building a Market-Friendly Middle Class," remarks to the Annual World Bank Conference on Development Economics, Washington, D.C., April 18, 2000, at carnegieendowment.org; Walter Russell Mead and Sherle R. Shwenninger, "A Financial Architecture for Middle-Class-Oriented Development," Council on Foreign Relations Press, October 2000; Afshin Molavi, "Mortgage Markets Will Strengthen Arab Middle Classes," *Daily Star,* September 17, 2004; Glenn Yago, Betsy Zeidman, and Bill Schmidt, "Creating Capital, Jobs and Wealth in Emerging Domestic Markets: Financial Technology Transfer to Low-Income Communities," Milken Institute policy brief, January 2003.

27. For an earlier version of this argument, see Anatol Lieven, "A Difficult Country: Pakistan and the Case for Developmental Realism," *National Interest,* Spring 2006.

28. *2006 National Trade Estimate Report on Foreign Trade Barriers,* Pakistan chapter, issued April 3, 2006; "Pakistan Exports to US Up 13.2 Per Cent in 2005," *Daily Times* (Lahore), April 3, 2006; see also K. Alan Kronstadt, "Pakistan-U.S. Relations," Congressional Research Service issue brief for Congress, January 28, 2005.

29. For U.S. aid to Pakistan, see "USAID/Pakistan" at www.usaid.gov/pk.

30. Stephen Philip Cohen, *The Idea of Pakistan* (Washington, D.C.: 2004, Brookings Institution), p. 313.

31. See Lieven, "A Difficult Country." For the background to U.S.-Pakistani relations, see Cohen, *The Idea of Pakistan;* Dennis Kux, *The United States and Pakistan, 1947–2000: Disenchanted Allies* (Baltimore: Johns Hopkins University Press, 2001); Owen Bennett-Jones, *Pakistan: Eye of*

the Storm (New Haven: Yale University Press, 2002); Hassan Abbas, *Pakistan's Drift into Extremism: Allah, the Army and America's War on Terror* (London: M. E. Sharpe, 2004); Hussain Haqqani, *Pakistan: Between Mosque and Military* (Washington, D.C.: Carnegie Endowment for International Peace, 2005); Teresita C. Schaffer, "US Influence on Pakistan: Can Partners Have Divergent Priorities?," *Washington Quarterly*, Winter 2002; Anatol Lieven, "Preserver and Destroyer," *London Review of Books*, January 23, 2003.

32. For a grimly convincing picture of what is likely to happen to the Arab world if it fails to develop, see the United Nations Development Program's *Arab Human Development* report of 2003, at www.undp.reports .org.sa/reports.

33. For another version of the concert idea, framed as a "Gulf Regional Security Forum," covering the Persian Gulf rather than the Middle East as a whole, see Michael Ryan Kraig, "Forging a New Security Order for the Persian Gulf," *Middle East Policy* 12, no. 1 (Spring 2006). See also the report on the conference "Alternative Strategies for Gulf Security," *Middle East Policy* 11, no. 3 (Fall 2004).

34. From *Ayman Al Zawahiri, Knights Under the Prophet's Banner*, trans Foreign Broadcast Information Service, cited in Peter Bergen, *Osama bin Laden*, p. 389; see also Christopher M. Blanchard, "Al Qaeda: Statements and Evolving Ideology," Congressional Research Service, report for Congress, November 16, 2004.

35. See also Bruce Lawrence, ed., *Messages to the World: The Statements of Osama bin Laden*, trans James Howarth (New York: Verso, 2005); Max Rodenbeck, "Their Master's Voice," *New York Review of Books*, March 9, 2006.

36. See John C. Hulsman, Judith Kipper, Ambassador Richard Fairbanks, and William Schirano, "A Window of Opportunity," *Middle East Track II Peace Plan*, January 21, 2004. For recommendations that have partially inspired our own, see the 2004 Geneva Accord at www.cartercenter .org/doc1739.htm.

37. For Olmert's plans in this regard, see Chris McGreal, "Israel Unveils Plan to Encircle Palestinian State," *Guardian*, February 8, 2006. For the risk that the United States might support this, see Harvey Morris, "U.S. May Support Unilateral Israel Line," *Financial Times*, March 31, 2006.

38. For an earlier version of this argument, see Joseph Cirincione and Anatol Lieven, "Rethinking the Iraq Exit Strategy," *International Herald Tribune*, May 17, 2004.

39. For arguments in support of such a limited withdrawal from full hegemony, see John Deutsch, "Time to Pull Out, and Not Just from Iraq," *New York Times*, July 15, 2005; Lawrence Korb and Brian Katulis,

"Strategic Redeployment," Center for American Progress, September 29, 2005, at www.americanprogress.org.

40. See Peter Galbraith, "Bush's Islamic Republic," *New York Review of Books,* August 11, 2005; David Hirst, "Iran and Israel Will Be Kings of the Middle East Jungle," *Guardian,* January 13, 2006; International Crisis Group, "Iran in Iraq: How Much Influence?," *Middle East Report,* no. 38, March 21, 2005.

41. Flynt Lverett, "The Gulf Between Us," *New York Times,* January 24, 2006.

42. For suggestions of a previous Iranian approach along these lines, see the essay by the then Iranian foreign minister, Kamal Kharazi, "The View from Tehran," in *Middle East Policy* 12, no. 1 (Spring 2005).

43. Niebuhr, *The Irony of American History,* p. 146.

44. See The International Crisis Group, "Iran: Is There a Way Out of the Nuclear Impasse?" *Middle East Report,* no. 51, February 23, 2006; Marco Vicenzino, "Iran: The Impending Crisis," *Global Views,* January 12, 2006.

45. See Carne Ross, "Could Sanctions Stop Iran?," *Washington Post,* March 30, 2006; "Head of Russia's Iran Studies Center Says Tehran 'Not Scared' of Sanctions," Interfax, March 12, 2006.

46. National Security Strategy (NSS) 2006, pp. 12, 20, 38.

47. Richard Clarke and Steven Simon, "Bombs That Would Backfire," *New York Times,* April 16, 2006.

48. Mark Perry and Alastair Crooke, "How to Lose the War on Terror," *Asia Times,* March 31, 2006.

49. See Ray Takeyh, "A Profile in Defiance," *National Interest,* Spring 2006; Karim Sadjadpour, "Behind Iran's Hard Line on Israel," *Boston Globe,* December 23, 2005.

50. See Guy Dinmore, "Bush Enters Iran 'Freedom' Debate," *Financial Times,* March 31, 2006.

51. See the various statements included in "A Shia Crescent: What Fallout for the United States?," conference of the Middle East Policy Council, Washington, D.C., October 14, 2005, chaired by Ambassador Charles Freeman, with Juan Cole, Kenneth Katzman, Karim Sadjadpour, and Ray Takeyh.

52. Quoted in Peter Galbraith, "The Mess," *New York Review of Books,* March 9, 2006.

53. See Dana Priest, "Attacking Iran May Trigger Terrorism," *Washington Post,* April 2, 2006; Gary Sick, "U.S. Policy Toward Iran," statement before the House Committee on International Relations, February 16, 2005. See also Anthony H. Cordesman and Khalid R. Al-Rodhan, "Iranian Nuclear Weapons?: The Options If Diplomacy Fails," Center for

Strategic and International Studies, April 7, 2006, at www.csis.org/media/csis/pubs/060407_irannucoptions.pdf.

54. See John C. Hulsman, "United States Policy Toward Iran—Next Steps," testimony before the House International Relations Committee, March 8, 2006.

55. See Christopher de Bellaigue, "New Man in Iran," *New York Review of Books*, August 11, 2005; and the International Crisis Group report, "Iran: What Does Ahmadi-Nejad's Victory Mean?," *Middle East Briefing*, no. 18, August 4, 2005; Reza Aslan, "For Iranians, It Was the Economy, Stupid," *Los Angeles Times*, July 3, 2005.

56. See Roy Mottahedeh, *The Mantle of the Prophet: Religion and Politics in Iran* (Oxford: Oneworld, 2000), pp. 215ff, 370, 386; Janet Afary, *The Iranian Constitutional Revolution, 1906–11* (New York: Columbia University Press, 1996).

57. See Clifford Kupchan, "Iranian Beliefs and Realities," *National Interest*, Fall 2005.

58. See Najmeh Bozorgmehr, "Satellite TV Brings Iran a Sense of the Ridiculous," *Financial Times*, January 24, 2006; Najmeh Bozorgmehr and Gareth Smyth, "Bush's Farsi-Call Intervention," *Financial Times*, February 6, 2006.

59. Mottahedeh, *The Mantle of the Prophet*, p. 381. Gary Sick, conversation with the author. For some examples of how this game is played out in practice when it comes to contesting and managing elections, see Abbas William Samii, "Dissent in Iranian Elections: Reasons and Implications," *Middle East Journal* 58, no. 3 (Summer 2004). For the theocratic element in the Iranian state system, see Juan Cole, *Sacred Space and Holy War: The Politics, Culture and History of Shi'ite Islam* (London: I. B. Tauris, 2005), pp. 189–211. For vivid portraits of contemporary Iranian society and public attitudes, see Afshin Molavi, *The Soul of Iran* (New York: W. W. Norton, 2002), and Christopher de Bellaigue, *In the Rose Garden of the Martyrs: A Memoir of Iran* (New York: HarperCollins 2004).

60. See Stefan Wagstyl and Tom Warner, "Ukraine Rejects Orange Leaders," *Financial Times*, March 27, 2006; and Steven Lee Myers, "Reform Leader Suffers Setback in Ukraine Vote," *New York Times*, March 27, 2006.

61. For analysis of the background to the 2006 Ukrainian elections, see Yulia Mostovaya, "Choosing or Losing," *Zerkalo Nedeli* (English edition), March 25, 2006, at http://www.mirror-weekly.com/nn/show/590/52968/); Mary Dejevsky, "So What Went Wrong with the Orange Revolution?," *Independent* (London), March 28, 2006; "Year After 'Orange Revolution' Defeat, Ukraine's Yanukovych Is Back," Agence France-Presse, March 20, 2006.

62. For the Putin administration's emphasis on the treatment of Russian-

speaking minorities as a key test for Russia's relations with its neighbors, see Putin's speech in Baku, February 22, 2006: "Attitude to Russian Language Indicates Attitude to Russia" (Itar-Tass); and "Russia Wants to See Compatriots in Other Countries Enjoy Full Rights—Ministry," Ria-Novosti, March 8, 2006.

63. See "Nearly Half of Ukrainians Speak Russian at Home—Poll," Interfax, March 10 2006; Mara Bellaby, "Voting Could Move Ukraine Closer to Moscow," Associated Press, March 29, 2006.

64. For a semiofficial Russian reaction to NSS 2006, see Sergei Karaganov, "Russia-US: Back to Peaceful Coexistence?," in the governmental newspaper Rossiiskaya Gazeta, March 24, 2006.

65. Results at www.levada.ru. For other polls showing similar results, see Georgy Ilyichev, "New Poll Reveals Attitudes to Policy Priorities," Izvestia, March 30, 2006; see also "Most Russians Want a Continuation of Putin's Course After 2008," Interfax, March 29, 2006.

66. Neil Buckley, "Self-Confident State Re-enters World Stage," Financial Times, April 21, 2006.

67. See "Explaining Putin's Popularity," Untimely Thoughts' Weekly Russia Experts' Panel, introduced by Peter Lavelle and Scott Spires, March 17, 2006, at www.untimely-thoughts.com; and Igor Zevelev and Kirill Glebov, "If You Want Democracy, Don't Push Putin," International Herald Tribune, March 12, 2006.

68. For the Bush administration's emphasis on democratization in its dealings with Russia, see Igor Torbakov, Jamestown Foundation Eurasia Daily Monitor, March 28, 2006, "U.S.-Russia Relations: Growing Rift Over Eurasia's Democratization."

69. Quoted in Isaacson and Thomas, The Wise Men, p. 572.

70. For Senator Richard Lugar's report on the progress of this program as of August 2005, see http://lugar.senate.gov/nunnlugar.html.

71. For the radical Islamist threat in Central Asia, see Martha Brill Olcott, "Russian, Central Asian and Caucasian Threats: A Four Year Assessment," testimony to the House Committee on Armed Services Threat Panel hearing on Threats in Eurasia, September 22, 2005; Zeyno Baran, "Hizb ut-Tahrir: Islam's Political Insurgency," Nixon Center, December 2004.

72. For Russia's strategy linking energy and geopolitical influence, see M. K. Bhadrakumar, "Reheating the Cold War," Asia Times, March 24, 2006. For Russia's critical importance as an energy supplier to the West, see Alexander Rahr, "Big Politics by Gaslight," Trud, March 28, 2006.

73. For another argument along these lines, see Nikolas Gvosdev and Dimitri Simes, "Rejecting Russia?," National Interest, Summer 2005.

74. See Anatol Lieven, Ukraine and Russia: A Fraternal Rivalry (Washington, D.C.: United States Institute of Peace, 1999), especially pp. 153–61.

75. See Anatol Lieven, "Do Not Dismiss Putin Out of Hand," *Financial Times*, February 28, 2006.

76. In the longer term, as Michael Lind has recommended, Russia should also be invited alongside other post-Soviet states to become a full member of NATO, thus transforming it from an anti-Russian alliance into a pan-European security organization. Lind, *The American Way of Strategy*, p. 270.

77. The best analysis and most sensible recommendations concerning the frozen conflicts in Abkhazia, South Ossetia, and Nagorno-Karabakh are produced by Conciliation Resources, at www.c-r.org. The best regular reporting on these conflicts, and the unrest in the Russian north Caucasus, is by the Institute for War and Peace Reporting, at www.iwpr.net.

78. For recommendations on Western policy toward the Chechen conflict and wider unrest in the north Caucasus, in the general spirit of ethical realism, see Fiona Hill, Anatol Lieven, and Thomas de Waal, "A Spreading Danger: Time for a New Policy Toward Chechnya," Carnegie Endowment for International Peace policy brief, no. 35, February 2005, at www.carnegieendowment.org. For a warning of the threat of new hostilities in the Georgian separatist regions, see Liz Fuller, "Are Ingushetia, North Ossetia on Verge of New Hostilities?," Radio Free Europe/Radio Liberty analysis, March 28, 2006. For the Russian strategy toward these conflicts, see Simon Saradzhyan, "Russia Sees Kosovo as the Answer," *Moscow Times*, March 29, 2006.

79. For official Chinese views of the relationship, see Zheng Bijan (chair, China Economic Forum), "China's 'Peaceful Rise' to Great Power Status," and Wang Jisi (director, Institute of International Strategic Studies, Central Party School, Beijing), "China's Search for Stability with America," in *Foreign Affairs*, September–October 2005.

80. See David M. Lampton, "Paradigm Lost: The Demise of 'Weak China,' " *National Interest*, Fall 2005; Kenneth Lieberthal, "American Perceptions of China," National Committee on U.S.-China Relations, at www .ncuscr.org/articles.

81. For very valuable recommendations on U.S.-Chinese relations based on the concert idea, see Lind, *The American Way of Strategy*, pp. 271–73.

82. For hard-line neoconservative views of China, see Frank Gaffney, testimony to the House Armed Services Committee, July 13, 2005, at www.centerforsecuritypolicy.org/GaffneyChinaTestimony; William Kristol and Ellen Bork, "The Bush Administration, Taiwan, and China," *Daily Standard*, February 10, 2004. For a more moderate neoconservative approach to building an international alliance to contain China, see Thomas Donnelly, "The Big Four Alliance," American Enterprise Institute online, December 2, 2005.

83. Robert B. Zoellick, "Whither China: From Membership to Responsibility?," remarks to the National Committee on U.S.-China Relations, September 21, 2005, at www.ncuscr.org/articles; see also Richard Haas, *The Opportunity: America's Moment to Alter History's Course* (New York: Public Affairs, 2005), passim.

84. See Chung Chin Lee, "China's Rise, Asia's Dilemma," *National Interest*, Fall 2005. For likely European responses to increased U.S. military containment of China, see Robin Niblett, "China, the EU, and the Transatlantic Alliance," testimony before the U.S.-China Economic and Security Review Commission, July 22, 2005.

85. See Steven C. Clemons, "Navigating America's China Challenge," the New America Foundation, November 17, 2005.

86. See Lanxin Xiang, "Why Washington Can't Speak Chinese," *Washington Post*, April 16, 2006.

87. See Robert S. Ross, "A Realist Policy for Managing U.S.-China Competition," Stanley Foundation Policy analysis brief, November 2005. See also Michael O'Hanlon, "Conflict Scenarios over Taiwan: How to Avoid, or Contain, War," speech at China Reform Forum, Beijing, April 6, 2006, at www.carnegieendowment.org.

88. See Doug Bandow, "Seoul Searching: Ending the U.S.–South Korea Alliance," *National Interest*, Fall 2005.

89. For a moderate Taiwanese view of the situation, see Andrew Yang, "Taiwan Security Review: One Decade After the 1996 Missile Crisis," talk at the Carnegie Endowment for International Peace, March 23, 2006, at www.carnegieendowment.org.

90. See David M. Lampton and Travis Tanner, "Taiwan's Elections, Direct Flights, and China's Line in the Sand: Implications for Washington, Beijing and Taipei," Nixon Center, 2005.

91. See Barrington Moore, *The Social Origins of Dictatorship and Democracy* (Boston: Beacon, 1966).

92. Zoellick, "Whither China."

Acknowledgments

This book could never have been written without the encouragement, unremitting effort, and sound advice of our agent, Will Lippincott. We are deeply grateful to him. We also wish to thank the staff at Pantheon: in particular, Dan Frank, the editorial director; Marty Asher, both for his interest in our work and his help in improving it; Andrew Miller, for an inspired job of editing; and Katie Freeman, for all her hard work in publicizing the book. Nicholas Gvosdev, Ximena Ortiz, and the staff of *The National Interest*, published the original essay on which this book is based, and have provided an irreplaceable forum for searching and open debate on international affairs. Some of the ideas expressed in this book were expressed first in Anatol Lieven's op-eds for the *Financial Times*, which he regards as the premier journal of the world community.

Anatol Lieven would like to thank his institute, the New America Foundation of Washington D.C. and Sacramento, for its unstinting support, and his colleagues there for their intellectual inspiration and comradeship. In particular, he is indebted to Steve Clemons and Sherle Schwenninger for their confidence and essential help. Erica DeBruin, Alexander Konetzki, and Sameer Lalwani assisted enormously with the research and worked intensively to very tight deadlines. Anatol Lieven has benefited over the years from interaction with many people in the foreign policy world, but would like to single out Owen Harries, former editor of *The National Interest*, as a profound influence and a generous friend.

As always, he gives his love and gratitude to his wife, Sasha, for her kindness and patience during the writing of this book; and to his son, Misha, in the hope that his generation will not suffer from the crimes and errors of today.

John Hulsman would like to thank with deepest affection and gratitude his "Band of Brothers (and Sisters)." In particular, Ewan Watt, Shora Zamani-Fekri, David Chambers, and Will Schirano have imbued this project with an almost feudal zeal that has been contagious. Thanks for helping create the open, demanding, rigorous, brave, committed, and (well, yes) fun intellectual climate that has made this book what it is. I shall always remember where I was on St. Crispen's Day . . . I was with you. May this book be a contribution to reminding America of what it once was, and what it can be again.